Your Towns and Cities in the (

# Ashton-under-Lyne
# in the Great War

Dedicated to Colin Barton of the Royal Welsh Fusiliers killed in action on 6 November 1917 during the Third Battle of Gaza, to the 1,510 Ashton men who made the supreme sacrifice, and to all those from Ashton who fought so valiantly in the 'war to end all wars' 1914-1918.

Colin Barton, I never knew you but I owe you my life. If you had not died, your widow, my grandmother, would not have married my grandfather. I appreciate how much you sacrificed for others and you gave me and my siblings a chance of life. The world may not be a much better place now but we have enjoyed it. Thank you.

Your Towns and Cities in the Great War

# Ashton-under-Lyne in the Great War

Glynis Cooper

Pen & Sword
**MILITARY**

First published in Great Britain in 2015 by
PEN & SWORD MILITARY
*an imprint of*
Pen and Sword Books Ltd
47 Church Street
Barnsley
South Yorkshire S70 2AS

ISBN 978 1 47382 313 6

A CIP record for this book is available from the British Library

Printed and bound in England
by CPI Group (UK) Ltd, Croydon, CR0 4YY

Typeset in Times New Roman by Chic Graphics

*Pen & Sword Books Ltd incorporates the imprints of*
Pen & Sword Archaeology, Atlas, Aviation, Battleground, Discovery,
Family History, History, Maritime, Military, Naval, Politics, Railways,
Select, Social History, Transport, True Crime, Claymore Press,
Frontline Books, Leo Cooper, Praetorian Press, Remember When,
Seaforth Publishing and Wharncliffe.

*For a complete list of Pen and Sword titles please contact*
Pen and Sword Books Limited
47 Church Street, Barnsley, South Yorkshire, S70 2AS, England
E-mail: enquiries@pen-and-sword.co.uk
Website: www.pen-and-sword.co.uk

# Contents

# Acknowledgements

With grateful acknowledgement to Pen & Sword for initiating and publishing this book; to the friendly and helpful staff of Tameside Local Studies in Ashton, whose interest and assistance in this project proved invaluable, especially to Sue Essex for her time and generosity; and to family and friends for accepting without rancour being totally ignored while I completed this book. Thank you everyone.

# CHAPTER 1

# 1914

Today, Ashton-under-Lyne, known locally as just Ashton, is hardly a separate place from the townships surrounding it. Collectively the area is known as Tameside, which is considered to be part of the Greater Manchester conurbation. Tameside is a Metropolitan Borough and comprises Ashton, Stalybridge, Hyde, Hattersley, Hurst, Mossley, Hooley Hill, Carrbrook, Audenshaw, Dukinfield and Droylsden. However, at the time of the Great War, Tameside MBC did not exist and Ashton was very much a town in its own right with a population of some 44,000 people. In earlier times its main distinction seems to have been the Nico Ditch, a defensive earthwork built in a futile attempt to repel Viking invaders. Since medieval times, Ashton has been a parish that was centred on Ashton Old Hall, originally the seat of the de Asshetons. Before the Industrial Revolution, Ashton was dismissed as 'bare, wet and almost worthless', a rather harsh description since the small rural villages around Daisy Nook and Ashton Moss were attractive enough in their own way and the old hall was a beautiful and imposing edifice set in its own large grounds. Today the hall no longer exists and its spacious gardens are lost beneath a car park, while Ashton Moss has virtually disappeared under an assortment of motorways, modern industrial estates and a massive blue box bearing the name IKEA. This book will focus on Ashton and not its near neighbours because in the early years of the twentieth century the towns were still distinct individual units and not subsumed into either each other or Greater Manchester.

By 1914 Ashton was very much an urban landscape and considered itself both a mill town and a garrison town. In 1881, the 63rd and 96th Foot Regiments merged to become the renowned Manchester Regiment, which was based at the Ladysmith Barracks on Mossley Road in Ashton. The regiment was known locally as 'the Manchesters' and remained at the Barracks until 1958, when they became part of the King's Regiment. There were four battalions: the 1st, 2nd, 3rd (Reserved) and 4th (Extra Reserve) Battalions. The regiment also included a number of Territorial Force battalions. The 1/9th and 2/9th Battalions were formed and based at the Armoury just off Old Street in Ashton. There were also the 11th, 12th and 13th (Service) Battalions formed and based in Ashton as well. Unlike its near neighbour, Glossop, seven or so miles away, Ashton was neither insular nor rural, but much more cosmopolitan. It had a cotton industry, where the mills normally worked a fifty-five-hour five-and-a-half-day-week, and a thriving hatting industry. Although there were farms in the surrounding villages and Ashton held an annual agricultural show each July, there was not the same emphasis on farming nor interest in allotment growing and managing vegetable blights as in the much more rural Glossop.

There were strong political elements in Ashton, with a big Liberal following, and locals were reasonably aware of the outside world and what was going on in it. The wide interests and outlook of the town was reflected in its local newspapers. The 'European question' had been discussed in the *Ashton Reporter* and Asquith's remarks about 'a situation of great gravity' had not been dismissed as simply alarmist. Ashton folk, however, did not let it interfere with their daily life and routines.

July 1914 began with a massive thunderstorm, the culmination of a recent heatwave. Some subsequently wondered if it was a portent of things to come. The Rose Day Festival took place on 4 July as usual, followed by the Ashton Agricultural Show on the 11th, which was attended by over 6,000 people. The town said goodbye to one of its citizens, Katie Boylan. She had been the captain of the local boys brigade, the only lady captain of a boys brigade in England, and she was emigrating to Canada to join her sister. On 1 August, Sir Max Aitken, the well-respected local MP, who would later become the newspaper magnate Lord Beaverbrook, held a public meeting to speak on a number of issues, which included the verbal abuse of King George V over the question of Home Rule for Ireland, that were being printed by the Radical Press. Meanwhile, Ashton Territorials were contemplating their annual two weeks employment which, this year, was to be in Carnarvon. The *Ashton Reporter* had continued to keep its readers informed about the European situation and so the declaration of war on 4 August came as a shock, but not a surprise, to the people of Ashton.

Things happened quickly. All railway excursions were cancelled for Ashton Wakes (the annual holiday for workers when mills and factories closed down for a week) which had been due to start on 15 August. A few local people who had been caught out by being in Germany at the outbreak of war were safely repatriated. A German visitor was arrested at the Portland Hotel in Ashton. Although he was a registered alien he was still sent to court under the new Restriction of Aliens Order. The Territorials did not go to Carnarvon but were mobilised for the first time in their history. A thousand men reported to Ashton Barracks. Naval reservists in the town were instructed to leave for the naval depots. Ashton ambulance men volunteered for the Home Hospital Reserve. Ashton post office opened all night to pay the Reservists their 3/- (around £6.46 in modern values) pay advance. An Ashton minister condemned the war as 'a black crime against humanity' and a pacifist speaker on Ashton Market was silenced by heckling plus the singing of patriotic songs and the National Anthem by the crowd. Everyone thought it would probably not be a long war. It was just two countries, Germany and Austria-Hungary, with the help from the Ottoman Empire, against five countries, Great Britain, France, Belgium, Russia and Serbia. The problem was that the two main aggressors were well prepared, equipped and mobilised, while the five defendants were caught on the hop, so to speak.

The cotton trade in general had never really recovered from the American Civil War, which had spelt the beginning of the end for the cotton industry. Ashton cotton trade, which had had a disastrous quarter from April to June and had suffered stoppages with subsequent compensatory payouts to workers of £1,094 (almost £48,000), had been facing a discouraging outlook at best, and now found that mills were closing prompting necessity for more relief measures. It was a 'black prospect for the Cotton Trade'. There was a run on the Ashton banks for wages, stoppage pay, and the funds of Wakes savings clubs. Ashton Savings Bank and the Co-operative Society opened early to deal with the demand. Hundreds queued at the Ashton Co-operative Society as it was dividend day on 8 August and over £10,000 (nearly £440,000) was paid out. A War Relief Committee was set up to try and alleviate the distress caused by breadwinners enlisting and the recession caused by the declaration of war in the cotton and hatting industries. By the end of August £3,500 (around £153,000) had already been subscribed to the War Relief Committee and a decision was made to join the National War Relief Fund. Local shops curtailed their evening opening hours to help the War Effort and Relief Fund. There was a rush to buy flour, although a public statement was issued insisting that food supplies were giving no cause for panic buying. Advice was given against hoarding food because there was absolutely no necessity to do so. But at the same time advice was also given that porridge should be substituted wherever possible for flour products. The Board of Trade fixed food prices but admitted that meat prices had 'risen slightly.'

Although many cancelled their holidays, local folk tried to make as much of the Wakes as circumstances would permit. But the black clouds of war hung over all. This Wakes became known as the 'Khaki Wakes' due to the Territorials and Reservists, who were 'Tommies in the making'. One Ashton writer summed the situation up thus:

*Armoury, Ashton, c1914 (courtesy of Tameside Local Studies).*

'Up until a fortnight ago the war cloud had only just begun to appear on the distant horizon and so far as we in this country were concerned it was not expected that it would entirely envelop us [...] but the cloud extended and we are under the full force of the terrible storm [...] this sudden deluge has completely disorganised all pre-arranged plans.'

Great pride was taken in the Ashton Territorials and the Armoury and they were given free tram rides, free baths at the swimming pool, and extra food. Nothing was too much trouble for them. Of the Manchester Regiment, 1,850 men left Ashton for Grimsby to travel to the Front. Irish couple Isaiah and Ana O'Grady had nine sons in the services, an amazing personal contribution to the defence of the nation. The local MP, Sir Max Aitken, was appointed private secretary to Andrew Bonar Law, the leader of the Conservative

Party, then in opposition. Ashton District Infirmary (now Tameside General Hospital) placed its resources at the disposal of the War Office and Ashton St John's Ambulance Brigade provided extra hospital accommodation in the Mechanics Institute on Church Street.

Ashton industry was badly hit by the declaration of war. Masons, Kershaws and Buckleys mills were the only ones to have kept working. But there came an upturn of work for the cotton mills, mainly due to the acute need for soldiers' and sailors' uniforms. Prospects of improvement had also come for the hatting trade, partly due to the forces requiring uniform hats and caps, but also picking up business because broken trade relations with Germany and Austria-Hungary created gaps in the market. The local council also borrowed £14,200 (over £621,000) for alterations to sewage and disposal works because not only would this benefit the inhabitants but it would also provide jobs for the unemployed. The local cinemas and the theatre tried to keep spirits up with the shows they offered. The Theatre Royal was staging *Anybody's Wife*, which had already had a good run in the provinces. *A Naval Secret*, *Bunny buys a Harem* and *Mabel's Nerves* were offered by the New Pavilion, while the Ideal countered with three 'big films,' which included *The Black Chancellor*, *Dublin Dart, The Irish Detective*, and *Lost in Mid Ocean*. The Queen's Electric was showing *The Arab's Prisoner* and the classic *Joan of Arc*. A hundred years on, the titles mostly seem rather childish and naïve, but in 1914 cinema was still in its infancy and movies were a great novelty. Films were silent so music was played, often on an in-house organ, using pieces to suggest the mood of the action on the screen. The stars of the day included Mary Pickford, Charlie Chaplin and Fatty Arbuckle. For the price of a few pence Ashton folk could lose themselves in the glitz and glamour of the picture house and try to take their mind off the grim realities outside the walls.

Ashton prided itself on being a barracks town, so when the national call to arms came, the town responded enthusiastically and there were record recruiting weeks. The local paper described the

*Stamford Street, Ashton, c1909.*

'rush to enlist' to 'teach the Hun a lesson'. Ashton New Moss Colliery (now lost under a massive B&Q store) held the record for the most war recruits after 25 per cent of its workforce enlisted. There had been early arrivals from Ashton at the Front and letters home described 'the terrific fighting around Cambrai.' A month after the war started, Ashton received news of the first fatality from the town. Captain Walter Mellor was killed on active service at the Front. Messages of sympathy from King George V and Queen Mary were sent to his parents. Ashton Corporal A. K. Butlin wrote of 'the thrilling story of fighting in France [...] Mons and Cambrai [... ] it was Hell let loose.' Private William Tobin of the 2nd Battalion of the Manchester Regiment, home on leave while his wounds healed, spoke of 'the terrible fighting at the Battle of Mons and [...] the trenches that were their own graves [for the British soldiers]'. The Ashton Battalion of Territorials had now left for Egypt. Sergeant Major Thomas was forming a military company of men, of a minimum height of 5ft 6 ins (about 1.75m), to be trained and be self supporting. One thousand Ashton sportsmen were to train for drill, musket practice and home defence. Roads and footpaths around the

Swineshaw Valley and Chew Valley to Crowden were closed as per military instructions. There was much talk of stopping local football matches but, although some clubs were abandoned, League officials took the view that games should go on and that players should assist the relief funds.

By mid-September, the Ashton Distress fund stood at £5,420 (just over £237,000) and there had been 470 applications. There was also a clog fund for those suffering hardship and 600 children were being fed in school canteens. The chief constable distributed 140 loaves and 190 pieces of meat to 'the needy poor'. He also gave ten guineas (£10 10s, approximately £460) from the proceeds of ticket sales from the council versus the police cricket match to Ashton District Infirmary. The match had been abandoned due to the war, but the gate receipts were kept and donated. There were various fundraising efforts. Miss Kenworthy raised £20 (just under £90) for the Belgian refugees who were beginning to arrive in the town, £100 (£4,375) was given to the Relief Fund from the Lodge Fidelity Freemasons in Ashton, and Ashton teachers gave about half that amount each month. Waverley Lodge Masons donated £25 (£875) to Ashton War Fund. There were collections for clothes funds and the clog fund. The scouts collected clean white newspapers for re-pulping. The distribution of relief and the numbers of destitute families were now causing serious concern in the town.

As the war tightened its grip, local tram services were curtailed as a further economy measure and this affected workers. The District Infirmary drafted in 120 extra nurses for a month's duty. Relief fund disbursements were now running at £388 (nearly £17,000) a week and 1,000 people were in receipt of relief ranging from 2s 6d (£5.50) to 12s 6d (£27.50), so more assessors were need for relief applications. The Ashton cotton industry was in a terrible state generally. For the last six weeks Ashton Weavers Association had paid out £5,000 (nearly £219,000) in unemployment benefit. It was policy only to pay benefit for a six-week period and it was a great drain on the unions, of which 300 members received their final payment and had to turn elsewhere for help. A thousand card room employees were affected by mill stoppages, which were due to lack of trade and a shortage of raw material. Fifty per cent of Ashton Spinners Union were unemployed. They received benefits for twenty-six weeks and the union was paying out £500 (nearly £22,000) every week. Trade union books of the time show 50 per cent unemployment across the board in the Ashton cotton industry. The local hatting industry was also suffering. There was short-time working both at Booth and More and at Wilde and Booth. Carrton and Co had closed and the body-making departments at Moores and Lees Broadbent were still closed. The Ashton Relief Fund was, however, well-supported by local efforts and around £450 (£20,000) was raised in just one week. Even the local children helped. The Empire Hippodrome complemented all this hard work by booking *Patriot Band*, eight instrumentalists, to play patriotic music for the people of Ashton, perhaps including the Manchester Regiment 'anthem' known as *The good old Manchesters*.

Ashton Armoury was recruiting to form a second Territorial battalion for home service. Mr G. Fletcher, the librarian at Ashton Library, which stands next door to the Armoury, placed a large scale map of French war hostilities in the library for the general interest of the townspeople. The recruiting at Ashton Barracks for the 14th Battalion Manchester Regiment was nearing completion and drafts were sent to Eastbourne to join the battalion. Whole families joined up. In Ashton, the McDermott family and the McCluskey family each had a father and his three sons on active service. The Broadhurst family sent three sons and a son-in-law to the Front. The Speers family had four sons and three nephews in the forces. The Coop family had four sons serving. And Mrs Duke, who could not walk, also had three sons on active service. Ashton Crimea veteran, Thomas Egan, aged 76, came to offer his services as well. 'I cannot stand idly by,' he is said to have told the recruiting sergeant. All the accommodation at the barracks was now required by the military, so soldier's wives and children had to move out and this caused great hardship in many cases in terms of the shortage of alternative accommodation and general moving expenses.

Bonfires were banned in Ashton for the celebration of Guy Fawkes in 1914 and so were public firework displays. The schools were, however, allowed to celebrate Trafalgar Day on 21 October. Belgian refugees had begun arriving in the town with lots of horrific tales to tell. They were housed in the Franciscan Convent, the New Jerusalem Schools and at a house on Mossley Road. The Belgian Refugee Fund was doing well in Ashton and in the Ashton area of Lancashire £12,000 (£525,000) was donated to the fund. However, returning or wounded British soldiers 'having shown great bravery under fire', got no official help or recognition like the Belgian soldiers. Where the Tommies were concerned there was nothing but 'a big gap'. The Tommies didn't particularly resent the Belgians, they too had shown great courage and had fought hard. They simply felt that the authorities should recognise their contribution as well. The returning wounded were cared at for Ashton District Infirmary, the Mechanics Institute, and at the Barracks. The need for more recruits was insatiable and the call went out. Ashton Barracks dealt with a rush of new recruits despite the terrible tales coming back from the Front. The new mayor, Councillor R. Wainwright, was to have a mayoral procession to celebrate his inauguration and churching in late November and, for the first time in their history, the 9th Ashton Battalion of the Manchester Territorials would not be present because they were on active service in Egypt.

Shops in Ashton demonstrated their patriotism by decorating their windows with photographs, sketches and curios of the war. A tailor's shop on Stamford Street put a Waterloo medal in its window, a shop in Old Street displayed a German helmet and bayonet while another shop nearby had managed to find a Ghurka's 'kukar', the Ghurka curved knife used as a weapon of war. Over 100,000 Ghurkas fought in the Great War, although they did not come from Ashton. Ashton Market, at that time one of the largest outdoor markets in the country, was trying to attract extra custom because the tenants of the stalls had been unsuccessful in obtaining any reduction on the 33.3 per cent increase in rents since war began. Christmas was coming and the retailers were hoping for good customer spending despite the war. All Turkish and Egyptian subjects now had to register as aliens as well as Germans and Austrians. There was, however, some discrimination against legal alien immigrants and arrests were made. Carl Hoch, a former German citizen, who was a watchmaker and jeweller resident in Stamford Street, Ashton, was arrested but eventually released from internment in Shrewsbury with his papers endorsed 'Discharged from German nationality'. Despite this he lost business as a result and his family endured some hardship. Another three Ashton traders suffered similar fates. S. Kay, a watchmaker and jeweller, who also lived and traded on Stamford Street, was interned, although he was of Jewish not alien extraction. Carl Friedrich Ludwig Teudt, a leather merchant from Uxbridge Street, was interned as an alien as well, but he did have a very Teutonic name. So too did Carl

*Ladysmith Barracks, Ashton, 1915. (courtesy of Tameside Local Studies)*

Durbeck, a local confectioner. All three were released before Christmas but the damage had been done to both their reputations and their businesses.

As in most towns and cities in Britain at this time there were problems caused in Ashton by drinking, and this led to fresh calls for more curtailed pub hours. It wasn't just the men. General Smith-Dorrien pleaded with the wives of soldiers not to drink so much. There were also claims that army separation allowances were being squandered on drink by wives but, as someone in the Ashton newspaper said, allegations against the women were easy to make and hard to disprove. The army even went so far as to issue a new order for 'the cessation of separation allowances and of allotments of pay to the unworthy'. Two Ashton women were thus penalised but, as it turned out, quite unjustly. Publicans felt reduced opening hours would mean Ashton had fewer attractions to offer visitors, and they were quick to point out that Ashton had the largest number of pubs in the area but the lowest number of convictions per capita, especially compared to Manchester. Ashton only had 52.99 convictions for drunken behaviour per 10,000 of its population whereas Manchester had over double the number at 107.25 per 10,000. Ashton Licensed Victuallers Association felt that rowdyism and excessive drinking should be proved before curtailing licensing hours, although regrets were expressed that any public funds, such as welfare assistance, should find its way into pub tills. The local temperance societies, however, were quick to point out that even fifty-three drunks per every 10,000 folk was too many and someone wrote to the local paper saying that the fighting men at the Front had no alcohol at all and didn't grumble, so why couldn't the civilian population do the same? It also didn't help that David Lloyd George had recently condemned British working men as 'drunken shirkers', which was rather an unjustified slur but wasn't helped by the fact that heavy drinking was proving to be a national problem.

The call-up cry for yet more men was constant. There was a big recruiting drive held in Ashton in late November with a procession of 2,000 men and a larger gathering of 4,000 at the Empire

Hippodrome to listen to speeches by the Honourable G. H. Perley, the attorney general, Sir Max Aitken, the local MP, Mr W. Edge, the local chief recruiting officer, and Sir Frederick Cawley MP. It was 'an inspiring spectacle of local patriotism'. Ashton Armoury was still recruiting at the barracks and at the Boars Head office on St Michael's Square, although the Ashton Territorials Reserve Battalion was now at full strength. The enlistment of so many young men affected junior football clubs, scouts and boys brigades, especially St Mary's Boys Brigade who lost their drummers and many of their football team. Fit and healthy men over the forces official enlistment age of 45 were also encouraged to enlist, and Charles Anstill , aged 43, of Ashton joined the Royal Flying Corps, an unusual enlistment for 1914. Arrangements were made for free medical attendance and medicines for Ashton soldiers and sailors and their dependants, and Ashton Relief Committee paid reservists' dependants each Monday morning at the post office.

The war hung over the town like a huge, dark thunder cloud. Ashton Ladies Relief Committee distributed 2,000 garments to 500 local people so that everyone might have something decent to wear. They also carried out a house-to-house collection for the District

*Lake Hospital, Ashton, c1919 .*

Infirmary. Queen Mary Work Room had been established for women willing and able to work who would not accept the charity of the Relief Fund. The work mostly involved the re-modelling and renovating of old garments and the women were paid 10/- (about £22) per week. Many women shared the 'silent burden of the agony of not knowing borne by the women at home who contribute by keeping the home fires burning', and devoted their spare time to knitting and sewing socks, caps, comforters and other garments for soldiers and sailors away on active service. They also helped care for the Belgian refugees. There had been an upturn in the cotton trade due to the required manufacture of sufficient uniforms and 70 per cent of the mills were now working. Some mills were weaving khaki cloth. Several doubling firms were approached for tent duck to make tents and haversacks. A military officer came to Ashton commandeering horses. He took three from Ashton Corporation and two from Ashton Co-operative Society. Notice was given that Ashton households were to receive a parliamentary return, which all those eligible for call-up would have to complete. The Home Office sent out a circular stating that pigeons were to be used to convey messages for the Admiralty and the public were instructed to 'refrain from interfering with birds'. The local paper was now devoting two pages every week to 'thrilling battle stories.' Ashton Corporal William Haggard was excited to have his DCM 'personally pinned on him by the king', and to receive 'a little present' from the Prince of Wales (later Edward VIII).

Christmas was approaching and Ashton folk tried their hardest to get into the spirit of the festival. Ashton orphans received treats from the Santa Claus ship *Jason*, which were sent by children in America. There were Christmas wishes from the mayor and gifts for the troops from collections. The mayoress's fund for Ashton Territorials was handsomely supported. The Canadian government sent a gift for the poor of Ashton which included thirty-two cheeses, forty kegs of tinned salmon, 100 sacks of potatoes, and 49,000lb of flour. The king sent pheasants and hares for local wounded soldiers. Amazingly, Ashton traders reported 'business as usual' in furs, clothes, jewellery, music and house furnishings, but at the same time the 'war and thrift' drive seemed to be working for Ashton Savings Bank who reported an increase of £7,413 (around £324,500) in business. The bank was stable and its savings were the bulwark for its depositors, but the war was placing a great strain on financial institutions. It was a martial Christmas, however, and this was reflected in the military subjects of Christmas cards. The Pavilion elected to show war films throughout the festive period but the Hippodrome turned to a little light relief with *The Coastguard's Daughter*.

December 1914 was one of the wettest on record with rainfall of 5.82 inches (about 15cm) was recorded. The cotton mills took their usual official holidays on Christmas Day and Boxing Day but there were some more prolonged stoppages. The shops took the same holidays with New Year's Day in addition. There were a number of sports fixtures and some Christmas parties. Ashton District Infirmary was caring for about thirty wounded soldiers. Each of these soldiers received Christmas greetings from King George V and Queen Mary and there was a box of cigarettes for each one from Queen Alexandra, the king's mother. The Military Hospital at the barracks gave thanks for the Christmas gifts and donations received. Ashton Workhouse Hospital offered to accommodate a dozen wounded soldiers or sailors. Local children held a bazaar to raise funds for the Mechanics Institute Hospital. On the whole, however, Christmas was a quiet affair for this year. There were fewer carol singers, although there had been greater church attendances than usual, and fewer parties were held on Christmas Eve and Christmas Day. The festivities were subdued by the long shadow of the war and the absence of loved ones from homes and dinner tables.

After Christmas, there was a rousing send-off for the 200 members of the 9th (Ashton) Reserve Battalion, Manchester Regiment (Territorials) after spending the Christmas holiday in Ashton. As they left a third contingent of 200 Territorials arrived for a week's furlough. Many hoped against hope that this would be the last Christmas of separation from loved ones.

# CHAPTER 2

# 1915

Ashton welcomed the new year with 'chiming bells, booming guns, shrieking sirens, and tooting railway engines'. During the first week of the New Year local theatres tried to keep folk cheerful by putting on pantomimes. The Theatre Royal had *Dick Whittington* playing while the Empire Hippodrome showed *Cinderella*. At the Empress Skating Rink, Lady Aitken provided a New Year lunch of soup, beef hash, two vegetables and mince pies for the 1,700 children of Ashton's soldiers and sailors. After lunch each child was given a toy. It was said afterwards that the tramping of little clogs on the cobbles that day lasted for hours. The war, however, still cast a huge shadow. Lord Kitchener's recruiting campaign increased. There were smart advertisements stating 'Remember Belgium' and notices went up that read:

> *The Great Resolution for the Year*
> *I will be a man and enlist today.*

Although pressure to join the armed forces was great, initially recruitment was slow but, by the second week of the new year, Ashton set a recruiting record of 250 men joining up in one week. There had been stories about 'the fun and amusement in the trenches' from three Ashton brothers who joined up in 1914, but it was not encouraging news that the Manchester Regiment suffered heavy losses at the Battle of Mons where 900 men were killed, wounded or listed as missing. The king appointed the first Sunday of the new year as a day of united prayer for all troops. Twenty-two Belgian refugees arrived from Holland and were housed in the New Jerusalem School. There were appeals for food, coal and clothing for them. There were any number of appeals for the troops but all elicited a good response, and the mayoress's fund provided a Christmas dinner for all the Territorials serving in Cairo. St Gabriel's sewing party was making dozens of mufflers, dayshirts, nightshirts, socks, bedsocks, handkerchiefs and pillowcases for soldiers in training, on service or in hospital. The last contingent of Territorials in training arrived from Southport for their New Year holiday around the middle of the month and the railway station at Charlestown in the centre of Ashton was the scene of much joy and anguish. Training in platoons instead of sections had speeded up the process and soon these men would be on their way abroad to serve their country.

The local places of entertainment tried to keep the mood cheerful. *Pearl Girl* was playing at the Theatre Royal while the Queen's Electric showed a film called *The Ragamuffin*, and May Mars, a well-known singer of the day, performed at the Empire Hippodrome. Her rendering of *My Persian Garden* always brought roars for an encore. Real life, however, was getting grimmer. There was a great deal of controversy over the proposal by Stalybridge Tramways to take over Ashton Tramways for reasons of efficiency and economy. Although the two towns were adjacent with little distance between them there was still a great sense of individuality and pride. Food prices had risen by 20 per cent and many folk were having difficulties in making ends meet. Ashton and District Weavers Association were also having problems after the failure to obtain a grant for more than a sixth of stoppage pay. Since the start of the war the weavers had been earning only half pay on average anyway, due to short time working and stoppages caused by reduction in raw materials available and by loss of trade. The main reason for the failure to obtain the grant was that the workers had not been able to prove 'abnormal employment', because many mills worked from 8.30am-4.00pm anyway and others simply stopped on Saturdays. Folk worked as and when they could, and eagerly grabbed any overtime. This rush to earn as much as possible suffered a hiccup after a horrific accident at the Stamford Manufacturing Mill in Ashton. Fourteen-year-old Alice Gordon was sweeping up and got her hair caught in a loom. She was scalped and was on the critical list for quite some time before making an eventual recovery. After witnessing this dreadful accident many of her workmates were unable to return to the mill for several days. Ashton, Stalybridge, Mossley and District Master Carriers Association chose this time to announce an increase in their rates of 2/- (£3.50) per day due to the fact that they had all had horses commandeered for the war effort and because of rising charges by farriers. The carriers were also suffering from 'red lights' hassle. The Ashton authorities were content if a rear red light was shown on the carts but the county (Lancashire) authorities insisted that red lights must have stained red glass and they fined those who did not comply. Interest in the 10-year-old Ashton Trader's Association was waning as well and membership was declining due to the wartime trade and resulting depression.

January had also been a month of torrential rain. Rain fell on twenty-four of the thirty-one days of the month, the wettest day being Wednesday the 15th when 1.25 inches (about 4cm) of rain fell. Between 6.60-8 inches (15-20cm) of rain fell during the month as a whole and deluges were so heavy that the sewers flooded and caused even the local rats to evacuate their homes. Towards the end of the month, though, the clouds literally lifted a little. Ashton received food windfall gifts for the Ashton War Relief Fund from Canada, who sent another 200 bags of flour, 100 bags of potatoes and a consignment of salmon, and this was supplemented by a crate of cheese from New Zealand. Food prices still continued to rise and the flow of supplies from southern Russia was cut off by the closing of the Dardanelles. Despite all this, however, a Burns dinner was held in the George and Dragon where a skirl of pipes heralded the

*Cavalry near Barracks in Ashton, c1915. (courtesy of Tameside Local Studies)*

mayor and the advent of the haggis ('a great chieftain of the pudding race' someone wrote) with boiled 'collywap' (probably potatoes as haggis is often served with mash and neeps, or turnips, and bubbly-jock, or turkey cock). This all caused great confusion to a lone Japanese visitor named Mr Abe, but attempts at any explanation to him by local folk have not survived.

Military matters were never far from people's minds. An Ashton seaman told a vivid story about the naval battle in the raid on Scarborough in January by a German cruiser, which had decoyed a British patrol, and Able Seaman Osmund Phillips, an Ashton marine on the HMS *Gallant Glasgow*, played a part in the sinking of Von Speer's convoy off the Falkland Islands. The Mayor of Ashton was backing a campaign to bring German war trophies to the town in the form of two Howitzers known as the German 'Jack Jones'. The Ashton Battalion in Egypt, where they had been fighting the Turks, was being sent to Syria. A military train was manufactured in neighbouring Dukinfield for bringing wounded military personnel from Southampton to Ashton District Infirmary. It was 'fitted up with baths, pharmacy, operation theatre, cots for the wounded, nurses and officers quarters, cuisine and chef, electric reading and hand lamps at each bedside, and every really up to date convenience'. The Infirmary was doing pioneering work in pathology and dentistry and also possessed Rontgay Ray (X-ray) equipment. The pressure on beds for treating wounded soldiers and sailors increased and Richmond House, which had formerly belonged to the Lupton family, was made ready to treat fourteen patients. Schools and workplaces put up Rolls of Honour for serving members or ex-members who were in the forces, and Christchurch School already had the names of 140 scholars on its Roll of Honour. Ashton Education Authority insisted that patriotism be taught in its schools.

In early February it was decided to cancel the *Black Knight Pageant* due to take place on Easter Monday. The pageant was labelled inopportune and inappropriate in a time of war. The origins of the pageant are obscure but it evolved from a ceremony known

*Ashton District Infirmary, c1917. (courtesy of Tameside Local Studies)*

as *Riding the Black Lad* sometime in the mid-eighteenth century. The Black Knight was supposed to have been, or based upon, Sir Ralph de Assheton, who was born in 1422 and lived in the old hall around which pre-industrial Ashton had been centred. He attended the coronation of Richard III and was made lieutenant of the Tower of London. Sir Ralph rode a huge black horse and was said to have been a cruel man who ill-treated and terrorised his tenants. He was said to have had those who seriously annoyed him rolled down a hill in a spiked barrel. The real origins of this tale are not known, and there is no supporting documentary evidence for it, but there is always a grain of truth in folklore. The children of Ashton in particular were bitterly disappointed for the pageant was one of the year's highlights.

Ashton Corporation decided to take action now against defaulting ratepayers in order to fill its coffers. However many shopkeepers, hit hard by the war and the resulting trade recession, found it very difficult to pay. Ashton Farmers Association debated the problem of rising food prices, some of which were not caused by scarcity or withholding stocks but simply because less milking cattle were kept for dairy as the price of feeding stuff rose steadily.

This affected the supplies of milk, cream, butter and cheese. The fatstock (cattle kept for sale to butchers) market was booming by contrast owing to the ability to freeze meat, which meant it could be kept until prices were pushed up even more. The high price of feeding stuff was condemned as blatant profiteering. Ashton Corporation agreed to pay half of fixed wages to dependants of employees who had enlisted. However, if the dependants were also claiming separation allowance, the wages paid were reduced by the amount paid in separation allowance. A number of families were therefore forced to exist on half their previous income and this caused severe problems. However the War Relief Fund had been well-supported through donations and subscriptions so this was now closed as it had sufficient funds to deal with applications caused through war-induced financial hardship.

Parliament had passed a Defence of the Realm Act (DORA), which meant that the military authorities could take any action they deemed necessary in the national interests while the country was at war. From 1 March, it was decided that lighting had to be greatly reduced as a safeguard against potential aerial raids by Zeppelins, widely regarded as a 'pursuance of the German policy of frightfulness', after attacks on Kings Lynn and Yarmouth. The following actions were to be taken:

- a portion of the street lighting was to be extinguished
- other street lights were to be turned down, except in cases of fog
- illuminated and advertising signs were to be taken down
- the greater part of windows were to be shrouded
- lights alongside water, docks, river, canals, etc, were to be masked to prevent reflection
- lit roof areas were to be covered
- railway lights in stations and goods yards were to be dimmed
- lights were to be low in buses and trams
  groups of flares in streets or markets were prohibited

*Zeppelin airship in flight on the eve of the Great War, c1911.*

- powerful headlights were banned
- rear red lights must be carried by any vehicle or person using a public highway

If Ashton folk thought these measures were Draconian, they didn't say so but complied as best they could, although some grumbled about the potential for accidents as people made their way around in, at best, a deep gloom. The public were advised to familiarise themselves with images of British and German aircraft. German aircraft had wings that sloped or pointed slightly to the rear and their airships tended to be much larger than British airships. In case of attack people were told they should seek shelter in the nearest basement when enemy aircraft was sighted. They were also warned they should not stand in a crowd, touch unexploded bombs or fire at any enemy aircraft. Not everyone seemed frightened of the

Zeppelins. Decades after the Great War, Mrs Ellen Murphy reminisced about the night she had seen a Zeppelin over Ashton:

> I was never afraid [...] I remember standing at the door one night, and I thought, 'what's that roar?' I looked up at the sky and I saw the most beautiful thing I'd ever seen in my whole life. It was the length of a row of houses where I lived. It was every colour. It had come down that low and it was a Zeppelin. Everybody ran in and put their lights out. I didn't. I looked up and I thought 'Oh isn't it lovely!' (Voices of Ashton-under-Lyne. Southall, Derek comp. Tempus Oral History Series. 2000)

*Darkened Ashton* became a familiar headline in local papers and the main topic of conversation. Those with a good sense of humour said that dogs and prams should also have red rear lights and that prams should have a horn as well. Blinds and shades appeared in every window and all external lights were dimmed or shaded. The weather did not help. It continued wet and cold and local sport was played in 'storm and rain'. In March there were blizzards but for once this was seen as a blessing. Zeppelins saw Ashton as a target because it was 'a depot' for the Manchester Regiment. The blizzards prevented the Zeppelins from attacking. It was arranged that the steam siren at Ashton Gas Works would sound continuously in case of an air- or land-based attack. Ashton, as a garrison town, should then extinguish all lights and people take shelter in the nearest cellar. People in Ashton actually began suffering from depression (now recognised as SAD – Seasonally Affected Disorder) due to little or no murky light and 'the dense pall of rain that seems to hang continuously over the town'.

A rare piece of encouraging news was that separation allowances were to be increased and the numbers of those eligible to receive them broadened. Soldiers' wives now received 5/- (£8.75) per child instead of the former 2s 6d (£4.37). For two children they received 8s 6d (£14.88) and 2/- (£3.50) for each additional child. All allowances were payable for children up to 16 (instead of 14 as previously), and they were payable in respect of any child the absent soldier had been maintaining as a member of the household. Dependants were now defined as any person who had been dependent on a soldier or sailor, irrespective of whether there was a relationship. However, payments often had to be made without a proper address being given. The war was responsible for many changes of tenancies because, as breadwinners enlisted, families doubled up for the sake of economy. There were lots of empty houses and often any notifications sent would go astray.

Ashton Tipperary Club was formed as a social club for the wives and mothers of those serving in the forces. They met regularly for a programme of songs, music or a talk, followed by a tea and discussion of problems from which its members might be suffering.

There were local concerts, like those given to the wounded soldiers at the District Infirmary every Wednesday and Saturday, dances and events raising funds for the war, as well as for shirts, socks, underwear and vegetables for the Belgian refugees, and also for clothing for tuberculosis (TB) sanatoriums, which were fighting hard against the 'white scourge' that cost thousands of young people their lives every year. A war bonus was paid to municipal workers but not to tramways workers. This, of course, was to lead to the threat of strike action on the part of the tramways workers. The police also received a weekly war bonus. A local vicar voiced his annoyance that more fathers went to football on Saturday afternoons than attended his church on Sunday mornings because they were 'too prone to seek for sensational amusements'. It had been questioned whether sporting activities were rather frivolous to be continued during wartime, but there was a lot of interest, in football and cricket especially, and it was decided that good healthy outdoor activities were to be encouraged. The authorities also hoped it would keep boys too young to work or enlist out of trouble and give the men less time to spend in the pubs.

Although the weather was good and Ashton received 30,000 visitors over the period, Easter week was another subdued and overshadowed affair, especially without the Pageant of the Black Knight. A military band played in front of the Town Hall while the local theatres and cinemas did their best to raise spirits with some light-hearted films such as *Sir Galahad of Twilight* at the Ideal Palace and *A Texas Ranger*, a romantic Western shown at the Theatre Royal. Shortly after Easter the lighting restrictions in Ashton were withdrawn, although no explanation was given. The press complained about news blackouts and misinformation on the 'war for might or right', as they termed it. Soldiers had begun returning on leave, grim faced and exhausted, referring to battles in the Ardennes and at Mons and Neuve Chapelle (of which the local MP, Sir Max Aitken, gave such an eloquent account) in terms such as 'it's Hell! Hell! and Hell let loose!'.

Five doctors from Ashton joined the Army Medical Corps and local medical services were struggling to cope with their absence. New hygiene and sanitation regulations had finally wiped out smallpox and folk hoped standards would not be allowed to slip because of the short staffing. Patriotic fervour and help came from the most unexpected quarters and on 1 May, Rev'd Henry Parnaby, the pastor of the Albion Congregational Church in Ashton, started work helping to make munitions at a local factory in addition to his pastoral duties. He insisted on donating his wages to various war charities. Ashton Gas Company increased their output of Toluol to help in the manufacture of explosives as requested by Lord Kitchener. Toluol is a hydrocarbon of the benzine group and can be recovered from the manufacture of gas. It was used in making TNT shells, which were known as Jack Johnsons because of the black smoke caused by their explosion (nicknamed after the US boxing champion Jack Johnson, who was black).

Meanwhile, there was 'trouble at mill' again, although the reasons were understandable. Ashton weavers were suffering quite badly with higher food prices and lower compensation in wage terms. Fancy cloth looms were idle but plain cloth looms and weavers were fully occupied. Requests for higher wages were constantly refused as the trade was 'not profitable', according to employers. Weavers argued that a war bonus should be paid for plain calicoes and government orders, in addition to which the short-time working had reduced accident compensation payments and it was felt that victims should receive 50 per cent of normal pay rather than 50 per cent of wartime pay. It isn't known how much the unfortunate Alice Gordon received for being scalped by a loom but then, as now, if it could be proved that perhaps she was negligent she would have got nothing at all. The only matter on which it seemed that there was agreement was that, as 35 per cent of the male members of the Weavers Institute had enlisted, a Roll of Honour should be made. Some cotton mills were now on a fifty-hour week. The normal working week was fifty-five-and-a-half-hours, but many mills had previously only been working forty hours a week. There were also war bonus payments for employees at Jones Sewing Machine Company.

*Jack Judge, who wrote Tipperary, a wartime marching song, in Stalybridge near Ashton, c1915. (courtesy of Tameside Local Studies)*

At the beginning of May the May Queen was crowned and statues of the Virgin Mary were garlanded with flowers. It was a moment out of time when people could push the war to the backs of their minds and enjoy themselves, if only for a very short while. A week later reality kicked in hard again. The *Lusitania* was torpedoed on 7 May off the coast of Ireland and sank rapidly with the loss of 1100 lives. Mrs Bull and Mr and Mrs Burley, together with their children, of Ashton, were all drowned. Only Mrs M. A. Wyatt from the town was saved. There was outrage at the flouting of the wartime convention that civilian ships with women and children on board should not be attacked by the enemy. The bad news just seemed to go on and on. Butchers, badly hit by meat shortages, reduced their opening hours by closing all day Monday and Tuesday, and on Wednesday and Thursday afternoons. Library opening hours were reduced. All the male members of staff had enlisted and Ashton Free Library was staffed by female assistants throughout the war. Tuesday half-day closing was enforced for all businesses. Whit week approached and, once more, no one felt much like celebrating. In any case all railway excursions for Whitsuntide had been cancelled due to the war and trying to conserve resources. The Whit Friday processions by the Sunday schools went ahead, however, although they were dominated by khaki and by military music. The day itself was sunny, however, and it brought a little welcome relief. Stamford Park was praised for its facilities, its blooms, the 'real sand' provided for the children to play in and the pond where miniature boats could be sailed. People enjoyed walks and picnics. Four little girls took advantage of the occasion to make scent sachets and hair tidies, which they sold at a small bazaar to raise money for the Mechanics Institute Hospital. St John's Ambulance Brigade had a very successful collection for new beds at a French hospital. Ashton cricket team played a match with Dukinfield but Dukinfield dismissed ten of their batsmen for just eight runs. It was a brief interlude in the grim business of enduring the privations of war while waiting and worrying about loved ones far away. Two weeks later they were shocked by a letter from a wounded soldier, which appeared in the *Ashton Reporter*. He had read in the paper of the Whitsuntide celebrations. 'Do we realise the dangers of the Great Crisis?' he wrote. 'I was shocked at the scenes of revelry, picnics and wines [... in Ashton...] you should see how it compares to Flanders processions of frightened, sick, displaced children clinging desperately to their widowed mother's skirts.'

Ashton soldiers caught in what was described as the Ypres inferno talked of the first use of chemical warfare, the chlorine gas the Germans unleashed on them. One soldier described it: 'gripped by gas [...] horrible sensations of devilish German fumes like knives being thrust into the throat.' Ypres, it was said, was like a town of the dead. Ashton folk were becoming desperate for news of the 1/9th Battalion of the Manchester Regiment, but the Ashton Territorials were now in action for the first time and there were only desperate appeals from the front line for yet more men. Lieutenant Fred Jones, who had written regular dispatches, had been killed and this did not help the thirst for information. There were eager, desperate waits for casualty lists. Finally news filtered through that the Territorials were in the Dardanelles, fighting the Turks on the Gallipoli peninsula. Many Territorials had never realised that one day they might actually have to fight. Another 200 volunteers were needed immediately and maybe another 300 after that. Still too many men of fighting age in Ashton were not responding to call-up pleas. By the end of May, Italy had joined the war on the side of the Allies. There was a number of Italians living in Ashton, several of them naturalised. Recruitment was much to the forefront and they could provide an extra pool of able-bodied men. There were also calls for an artillery brigade to be formed in Ashton, which would consist of 600 men, seventeen officers, and three batteries of twelve guns. A lot of straight talking was aimed at the young men who paraded up and down Stamford Street saluting the pretty girls but who refused to enlist saying that they 'left all that sort of thing to other mothers' sons'. This annoyed people and there were a number of caustic letters to the local newspaper saying that the girls should ask them straight out why they wouldn't fight. Were they just cowards? There were also letters from incensed men serving in the front line saying that they resented having to fight so that folk like that could have the freedom to just walk away from the troubles. In like mind were letters to the cotton workers, pleading with them to call off their strikes and to support the lads at war who, at the end of the day, were earning a pittance, far less than the cotton workers who could work in relative safety and comfort without the constant threat of having their heads blown off. Finally, there was an angry dig at the severe drink problem that seemed to be affecting the whole country. Soldiers, said one at the Front, have no alcohol and feel that they are simply doing their duty. Why couldn't the folks at home just do the same thing?

Ashton was intensely proud of the Territorials, who now numbered 3,000 fighting men, and of the 2nd Battalion of the Manchesters from the Ladysmith Barracks in the town. It was the Territorials, however, who gave such a splendid account of themselves at Gallipoli. They were 'bearing up under a rain of shells and bullets' in the Dardanelles and doing 'grand work'. They charged through the Turkish trenches under heavy fire but many were killed, and Ashton mourned its losses. The local newspaper praised the 'Territorial Heroes in the Dardanelles' and published cheerful letters from some of them, which were used to encourage enlistment. Seventeen-year-old Private John Finnegan, who was killed in the Dardanelles, had organised his own Black Knight Pageant out there on Easter Monday and it had caused much amusement. Territorials machine-gunner Private William Shuttleworth, who died 'a heroic death' in the Dardanelles, penned a poem to his mother, which somehow survived:

*There is no distance that our love can sever,*
*Fairest hopes like ours span the longest way;*
*But my life is lonely, my heart is weary,*
*When I cannot see my mother day by day.*

A memorial service was held in Ashton Parish Church for the high numbers of Territorials who had been killed – forty in one day alone, thirty on another day. There was a civic procession and great solemnity and the funeral music by Chopin moved many to tears. The military hospitals were showered with gifts for returning wounded soldiers. The post office offered to send old books and magazines as reading materials for the troops to the Front free of charge. Wounded officers returning to Ashton to convalesce told of the 'bombs, bullets and shrapnel in Dardanelles fighting', while the local newspaper ran headlines such as 'A Thrilling Account of the Glories and the Dangers of the Bombardment of Turkish Forts' and 'Territorials capture Turkish trenches, guns and prisoners', while Able Seaman George Jones of Ashton explained the difficulties the British and French fleets and soldiers had to combat. Today the former trenches of the Gallipoli peninsula in the Dardanelles are

*Squadron Detachment 207 Armoury, Ashton, c1915. (courtesy of Tameside Local Studies)*

neat and clean, uniform and tidy, as though some giant hoover has recently smartened them up. There are massive memorials every few yards, many to Australians and Canadians as well but, despite everything that happened there, the horrors and the atrocities, there is a sense of peace as though the fighting spirits of a century ago have finally been laid to rest.

Back home a proud if grieving Ashton had other matters on its mind as well. The raising of an artillery brigade was underway. Recruiting was taking place at the Ashton Empire Hippodrome. The mayor concluded his recruiting speech with the assertion that 'girls prefer men with spurs'. Within a month the brigade was almost at full complement. The new brigade's official name was the Ashton Artillery Brigade – 181st Brigade (Ashton-under-Lyne) R.F.A. On the first day seventy-five men enlisted and by the end of July almost all of the required 718 officers and men had signed up. Another 170 men answered the Territorials appeals to enlist, perhaps spurred on by their achievements in the Dardanelles. However, another 200 were still needed. The loss of manpower was felt everywhere. There were now female tram conductors and female clerks in the railway offices as well as female library assistants and female teachers. The mills were forced to take on more women workers because there were just not the men to employ, and now there was talk of women working in the munitions factories. Ashton's response to supplying munitions workers had been better than Manchester's response per capita. There was also the matter of Lord Derby's Scheme of National Registration and its organisation to consider. This was to be a register of all residents aged 15-65, containing their names, ages, dates of birth, marital status, number of dependants and, most importantly, their current occupations. Two hundred and fifty enumerators were employed to deal with the fifty registration districts and 10,500 houses in Ashton. National Registration took place on Sunday 15 August when 33,000 forms were delivered to the 10,500 dwellings. There was, naturally in the circumstances, a preponderance of females within the required age range. It was necessary to fully utilise the nation's resources and the completion of the form was compulsory. It would also show possible enlisters. Failure to comply led to a £5 (£175) fine. The government was anxious to avoid national conscription, but quite prepared to do it if necessary.

There was debate as to whether a commemorative memorial service should be held to mark the first anniversary of the war. It was finally decided that a service should be held at St Marks. An appeal went out for cigarettes for the Territorials who 'get very miserable when there is nothing to smoke...' Someone made a list of consequences of the war, which included dearer food, no excursions, darkened streets, enforced economy, shortage of labour, reduced purchasing power of a sovereign (21 old shillings or £1 1s, approximately £36.75), but stated that it had all been taken reasonably calmly by Ashton inhabitants. There had been no riots, no special constables called-upon to uphold the law, no serious crime, and even drinking had been reduced. The major effect, of course, was the loss of so many promising young men, many still in their teens. That was the real tragedy, the real cost in human terms, and grieving families simply had to cope as best they could. There was further grief when the *Arabic* was sunk in a torpedo attack off Southern Ireland on 19 August. The ship sank quickly and Frank Tattersall, a well-known Ashton pianist, lost his wife and five-year-old daughter Irene. It was a very subdued Wakes at the end of August. A fair was held but even that was subdued. There was 'a singular absence of jollity and devil-may-care abandon [...] as though there were guilt at any sense of enjoyment' and 'a large number of catchpenny stalls but no circus or menageries or living picture booths or boxing [ ...] but then the modern fair is the product of the feverish haste of modern days' mourned one Ashton resident. 'Manifest delights have vanished into the limbo of the past.' The children seemed to enjoy it, however.

Ironically a slump in inquests for the month of September was reported in Ashton, but more heavy losses were reported among the Ashton Territorials. Forty men were killed in a single day. Captain

W. T. Forshaw was recommended for the Victoria Cross for bravery in action during 7-9 August on Gallipoli Peninsula in the Dardanelles. Two Ashton Territorials, Sergeant George Sylvester and Sergeant Harry Grantham, had also been awarded the Distinguished Service Medal for 'bravery, determination and endurance in combat against the Turks.' An Ashton soldier, Corporal W. Degnan, had also been decorated by the tsar for conspicuous gallantry in carrying messages under heavy fire. The king himself praised the Territorials for what the local newspaper had described as 'brilliant deeds by Ashton men in Gallipoli'. All the national registration forms had been collected and evaluated and its 'pink forms' showed there were about 5,000 men aged 19-40 (the main military age group) of fighting age in Ashton who were not in khaki. Men already in khaki were now requested to canvas those who were not. A recruiting rally was to be held for the Territorials, and the Volunteer Corps and the Civilian Corps were asked to help. Captain W. Edge, promoted from lieutenant for his services to recruitment, would be present. There was a great focus on this recruitment appeal succeeding.

Over half of the Ashton Tramways employees (thirty-nine out of seventy) had enlisted and this presented a staffing problem. With much misgiving it was decided that females might have to be employed by the Tramways Corporation but as conductors only. There was still a great reluctance to employ women to do the jobs that were traditionally seen as male enclaves, but mills, offices and shops were beginning to realise that they might have very little choice if they wished to keep open and working. The library was only kept open because of female staffing and there were now both male and female teachers. There was also a problem with low-paid apprentices who were still in training. The parents of those who enlisted were excluded from allotment pay but there was also a big question-mark over their servitude after the war. In fact, employment after the war, for those who had left jobs to enlist, was a major concern. However, unemployment among Ashton weavers had improved a little and the cotton wages dispute had finally been settled by an agreement to grant a 5 per cent war bonus from the beginning of 1916. The wages of cemetery workers and electrical fitters were to rise as well, and even the municipal workers managed to obtain a small pay increase. Food prices were still rising, but Ashton shopkeepers reported little grumbling, except about sugar, which was a government-controlled commodity, and price rises were used to try and discourage the use of lump sugar, which was now considered a luxury.

As ever the main focus was on recruiting men for call-up. 'No one must think that this war can be lightly won,' said one recruitment canvasser. The canvassing and button-holing of many men who appeared to be eligible for call-up was actually frequently embarrassing and distressing, for a high per centage of men who had tried to enlist were rejected on the grounds of physical defects. The list of defects for which would-be enlisters could be rejected shortened as the war went on, but sight defects could not be ignored. The Picture Pavilion emphasised the recruitment situation by showing a film called *Remember Belgium* at the same time. However, by the end of a two-week campaign, only 120 men had enlisted in the Territorials, and there were still 5,000 men of call-up age who had not done so. Although soldiers received free medical treatment and part-payment of their rent, the latter benefit was neither recognised nor practised in Ashton and this must have had some effect on willingness to sign-up. There was also still much heated debate about the question of married men or single men joining up first, and still much argument on both sides of the question. Public resentment was beginning to fester over the issue and at the end of September it spilled over when a shop selling game and vegetables belonging to Mr J. W. Salthouse in Ashton was attacked and looted, causing £10-worth of damage (£350). His 'crime' was to have eight sons, none of whom had enlisted. He protested that they 'were all good boys' and that 'folk were out to spite him', but in the climate of the time it was an inflammatory situation. Labourers were required by the Royal Engineers and these were recruited from men in the 40-47 age group, which was just above military call-up age. The pay was 3/- (just under £5) per day, plus the separation allowance.

Ashton had also raised two artillery units, the 181st Brigade Royal Field Artillery of 700 men, who were currently training somewhere in southern England, and the 143rd Heavy Battery Royal Garrison Artillery of 400 men, who were training closer to home in Blackpool. There were several fundraising appeals by both adults and children and a gratifying response to one for the Territorials by Mrs Garside that raised £434.14 6d (around £15,200). Ashton St John Ambulance Brigade sent 500 pipes, 125 half-pound (packs of tobacco about a quarter of a kilo), and 6,000 cigarettes to colleagues at the Front. Ashton & District Grocers Association arranged a number of social events for wounded soldiers and there was a concert for wounded soldiers at the Richmond House Hospital. In addition, there were appeals for gifts and comforts to send to the 13th Battalion of Manchesters serving in France, and lists of gifts for the barracks and the military hospitals. The mayoress's appeal for comforts raised £10 1s 3d (approximately £352). Sales of flowers and chocolates were the most popular method of fundraising for comforts. Nurse Amy Judson from Ashton, who was nursing Belgian soldiers in France, appealed for Christmas gifts to give to her charges to let them know that Britain was thinking of them and had appreciated their efforts at the Front. Lord Derby's Scheme carried on recruiting in the last week of October and signed-up 160 men, a four-fold increase on the previous week. It was a good response but there remained just over 3,500 men of military age in Ashton who had yet to enlist.

Guy Fawkes celebrations were still banned but sports and entertainment fixtures were kept up to try and raise morale. The Theatre Royal staged the international success *The Marriage Market* starring Dorothy Shale, a renowned actress of the day, and the Queen's Electric Theatre was advertising a great new novelty of talking pictures. It was reported that films could now be watched with vocal soundtracks, which actually synchronised with the film. Lieutenant William Forshaw, who had been awarded the Victoria

Cross, received his medal from the king at Buckingham Palace and was returning to Ashton to receive the Freedom of the Borough in recognition of his achievements. A new Union Jack flag was to be raised at this ceremony and the mayor called for bunting to decorate the Town Hall square and the surrounding streets. The Ashton newspaper reported on 'the unconquerable spirit of local men', assured its readers that 'Germans will never break through our lines' and ran a special review of the 'five months of magnificent work by the Ashton Territorials in the Dardanelles', including stories of 'Turks bodies piled high in front of the lines at the Dardanelles'. There were more honours for the Ashton Territorials when Lieutenant R. G. Wood was awarded the Military Cross for holding back the Turks. The 1/9th Battalion had now gained more honours than any other battalion in the Dardanelles for 'showing great gallantry and endurance' and in situations they had never expected to face.

There was now yet another debate on the question of the national drink problem. Someone in government had discovered that the alcohol bill of the country for the last six months of 1915 was greater than it had been in the same period for 1914. This could have been due to a number of causes but to people like David Lloyd George there was only one cause and that was the tendency of the British public at large to over-indulge itself with alcohol. There was, the local papers reported, said to be a particular need to curb drinking in Ashton. There were further calls for licensing hours to be restricted, despite protests from licensees, and the Liquor Traffic Control Board decided that a wide-ranging inquiry should be held, which would hear from all parties including the licensees. After all, if the population needed to defend itself against German invasion it would need to be sober to do so. As part of the war economy drive there was also talk of possibly curtailing shop opening hours. There were already shortages of meat and milk and reduced opening hours would help when supplies were restricted. Tuesday was traditionally half-day closing in Ashton, but recently a shopkeeper had been taken to court for opening on a Tuesday afternoon that had followed a bank holiday Monday. His defence was that the soldiers' wives who were paid separation allowances on Mondays were not paid until Tuesday if the Monday was a bank holiday. Therefore, he had opened to oblige and to allow them to do their shopping on Tuesday. The case attracted a great deal of sympathy but the contravention of opening hours was upheld. The Grocers Association supported his case but said that there should be either definite compulsion to close on Tuesday afternoons or definite exemption for those in certain trades.

December was a cold month and there was skating in Stamford Park after a hard frost had frozen the lake. The ice was 3 to 4 inches (8-10cm) thick. It had frozen over in late November for the first time and football matches were played on ice-bound fields. It was Christmas time again and many families in Ashton were facing a second Christmas without loved ones. The mayoress had already raised £10 (£350) toward the provision of Christmas dinner for the Ashton Territorials. This later rose to £90 (over £3,000). Tins of salmon, fruit, cakes, biscuits, toffees and soap were bought and sent out to the troops serving abroad. A 'pound day' was held at Richmond House Military Hospital when everyone was asked to bring a pound of something, either one pound in money (worth £35) or a pound of food for the larders. The Mechanics Institute Hospital, which had been praised as 'a real credit', acknowledged a number of gifts. Concerts for the wounded soldiers were given at the District Infirmary. Christmas comforts had been received by the 13th Manchester Battalion. Christmas parcels were dispatched to over forty prisoners-of-war. Ashton Tipperary Club, the social club for soldiers' wives and mothers, was very active and trying to take the women's minds off absent husbands, fathers and sons. There was a lower number of letters, cards and parcels to be delivered this year but twenty postwomen were hired to deliver them. Holly and mistletoe were scarce but turkeys and geese were in good supply. Toys were expensive. Ashton Workhouse, which had a total of 553 inmates (304 male, 249 female), a decrease of 128 on the previous year, was understaffed and basically being run by just two people.

Nevertheless they organised a Christmas lunch of roast beef and plum pudding for everyone, a nursery tea for the children, a tree with toys and sweets, and a carol concert. For the lunch 500lb (approximately 230kg) each of beef, potatoes and plum pudding were eaten. Lady Aitken entertained 3,000 children at the Pavilion with sweets and a film showing of *A Christmas Carol*. For children who regularly attended the Park School canteen there was a Christmas lunch of beef hash, boiled potatoes and Christmas pudding. The pantomime at the Hippodrome this year was *Dick Whittington*, appropriately enough, for the Ashton Savings Bank had finished the year in a strong position with a surplus of £9,413 18s 11d (about £329,500) and depositors invested in £50,000 (£1,750,000) of war stock. There was still optimism that the next year, 1916, would see the end of the war.

*Lake in Stamford Park, Ashton, c1913.*

The Lake, Stamford Park, Ashton-under-Lyne

# CHAPTER 3

# 1916

Following the wishes of the king, the church had declared that the first Sunday (2 January) of the New Year should be a day of intercession, a day of prayer, for all those fighting for 'right over might' and for their families left at home with the fervent hope that soon the war would be at an end. On the following Monday evening (3 January) a special Intercessionary Service was held at which all denominations came together to pray for a common cause. Those members of the 1/9th Battalion of the Territorials, who had received home leave in time for Christmas, spoke of having 'seen much, suffered much, lost much', in Gallipoli. Someone voiced thoughts for many when he said that the outlook seemed 'tinged blood red'. Christmas had been a quieter, more subdued affair than usual despite school parties for the children and entertainment for those in the hospitals. Folk were told they must be thrifty, although some newspaper wit commented that those who told others to be thrifty had never had to be, nor ever would be, thrifty themselves. In the two weeks before Christmas, more wounded soldiers from Gallipoli, and also from Flanders, arrived at the Lakes Hospital (part of the Infirmary). Bertha Mason, the president of Ashton Women's Liberal Association, was working in a rest camp and a British hospital in France. She had supported fundraising efforts for Ashton prisoners-of-war and had seen for herself some of the appalling conditions that the men in France had endured. Back in

Ashton, enlistment for immediate service had dropped, due in no small part to the raging debate of whether single men should go before married men, but there had been busy scenes at the attesting stations in December. Khaki armlets had now been given out to verify that a man had attested. There were forty-six groups under the Lord Derby scheme. Single men were grouped according to age in the first twenty-three groups. Married men were grouped the same way into the remaining twenty-three groups. Two thirds of eligible men in Ashton had now attested, ironically, more married men than single men, and were awaiting call-up. Medical examinations would be given to the men at that point. Wearers of attestation armlets were told to always carry Army Form W394 with them in case they were challenged by an officer, an NCO or the police. On 20 January, the groups two, three, four and five (of the Derby recruits) were called-up. Any claims for postponement or exemption, which was usually limited to six months, had to be made within ten days and would be heard by a tribunal. A few days later groups six, seven, eight and nine (single men aged 23-27 years old) were called-up.

The weather had turned very wet and now football was played in deluges of rain rather than on ice-bound fields. Those serving abroad had written to the local papers acknowledging their gratitude for the Christmas gifts they had received. In one part of France there were seventeen Ashton lads still serving altogether in the same group trying to keep up their spirits in the squelching mud of the trenches. Paper was in short supply and there was an effort to economise on its use. The *Ashton Reporter*, now reduced from twelve pages to eight in the name of the wartime economy, was sent abroad to France and the Dardanelles and provided a welcome link with home for the soldiers. War economies were reaching elsewhere too. Sunday postal deliveries and collections were curtailed. There were to be other restrictions as well from 17 January. Although there would still be full deliveries of letters and parcels at 7am and 1.15pm, there would be a restricted delivery at 6.15pm, and the 5.30am and 10.45am collections were to be suspended until further notice. One hundred years on and in peacetime this was still a postal service that can only be dreamed of now.

There was to be no road maintenance for the forseeable future. The cotton and weaving trades had not had a bad year in 1915 overall, but the cost of transporting 100lb (around 42kg) of cotton across the Atlantic had risen by six times as much. Ninety-eight per cent of weavers were now females. There were still various fluctuations in the items of cotton manufacturers, but that was only to be expected given the current situation. In addition, severe delays were experienced in railway goods traffic, which was causing concern to mills and manufacturers. Prices of sugar and flour had risen, but Queensland had sent £100 (£3,500) of foodstuff for the people of Ashton, which was a welcome New Year treat for the town. There was also a box of gifts for the local soldiers from Ashtonian folk in America.

Two lads were charged with stealing coal from the railway in Ashton. Coal fires were the main means of heating but coal was scarce and expensive. There was also the problem of considerable vandalism by local youths and boys. It was blamed mainly on the absence of fathers and the lax discipline of mothers. Measles was made a notifiable disease in a bid to stop the spread of epidemics and the benefits of quarantine were stressed, especially in times such as these when people needed to be as fit as possible.

Ashton Bible Society delightedly reported that the war had greatly increased interest in the bible and that ten million bibles had been handed out by the society over the whole country the previous year. One local soldier had more cause than most to love the bible for his copy, tucked into his uniform jacket pocket, stopped a bullet that would otherwise have killed him.

Ninety-three St John's Ambulance men passed examinations and 120 were sent to the Front, one as far as Salonika. The 6th Cheshire Battalion, which included men from Ashton and Glossop, was 'ready for the trenches'. The 1/6th Cheshire Battalion of the Cheshire Regiment Territorial Forces had been in France since 1914. The Gallipoli Campaign ended in defeat for the Allies and a victory for the Ottoman Empire, although the Territorials had fought against overwhelming odds, and it was a bitter pill to swallow after so much fighting and so many men had lost their lives. The Gallipoli peninsula was finally evacuated by the British Mediterranean Expeditionary Force, but the Territorials in Gallipoli were being refused leave even after eight months because of the sheer logistics involved in trying to get them home. Instead the exhausted and battle-weary troops were sent to Egypt or Mesopotamia. The one thing that had cheered them was the thought of the support of fresh recruits coming to join them, not fully realising the reluctance that had been shown by many potential enlisters. It would have been easy to dismiss those who were, at best, slow to join up, as cowards. But on the other hand, why would anyone show much enthusiasm for a situation where conditions were appalling and death far from home or a crippling injury was a common everyday occurrence? It was an incredibly difficult situation.

'Thrilling deeds by the youngest of a family of eighteen children' ran a newspaper headline. Private Walter Dewsnap had dashed into open territory seven times to rescue wounded comrades. His reward was to be maimed for life by a bullet and shrapnel that shattered his thigh bone. His mother had already lost fifteen of her eighteen children, although only one to the war.

The first groups of Derby recruits called-up had been attached to the Territorials. There had been a poor response by Ashton young men under the attestation scheme despite defaulters being liable to arrest and punishment. Only the physically unfit and munitions workers were exempt. David Lloyd George knew that the Derby Scheme was a last-ditch attempt to avoid compulsory conscription and it wasn't working. The Compulsory Call-up Bill had, therefore, already been drafted and gone for its second reading. On 27 January the Military Service Act was passed and officially sanctioned conscription for all men of 'military age'. The present year should, it was hoped, result in being the year of victory.

As if life wasn't miserable enough already severely restricted licensing hours were introduced for pubs and clubs. Ashton

*Cheshire Regiment 6ᵗʰ Battalion, Ashton, c1914. (courtesy of Tameside Local Studies)*

licensees made their case and pointed out that prosecutions for drunkenness had fallen over the past year and for the first time were down to two figures (ninety-three in Ashton's case). The mayor believed that drinking restrictions would only increase secret drinking by women. Juvenile crime was increasing and it was believed that this was because women were already too lax about discipline. Licensees felt it would ruin their trade and that there was no real cause for alarm about the amount of drink consumed. Their pleas fell on deaf ears. The Ban on Drink Order for Lancashire, Cheshire and Flint restricted the sale of alcohol in pubs, clubs and off-licenses to between 12-2.30pm noon and 6.30-9.00pm from Monday to Saturday, and 5pm-9pm on Sundays. Off-sales (off licenses) were to close an hour before the pubs and clubs each evening. There was also a No Treating order, which meant that people could not buy drinks for others. The temperance societies were absolutely delighted. The licensed victuallers protested that it would ruin them and their trade. The government believed it to be totally necessary for national efficiency in the war. Before the change in the law, public houses could be open from 5am until 12.30am. The drink restrictions were termed 'legislation gone mad' by outraged drinkers and licensees, but other voices claimed that if the cotton workers, or any other workers for that matter, were so hard up, then they should not be wasting money on drink. However, as more than one soldier pointed out, the troops had no alcohol at all and they weren't complaining, so the least the folks at home could do was to accept things with good grace.

January turned into February and the church celebrated Candlemas, the Christianised version of the old Celtic festival of Imbolc, the festival of the lambs. The Ashton Territorials were now resting in Egypt after their ordeal in the Dardanelles and the losses at Gallipoli. A number had been killed in the last days of action on that Front. One particularly tragic case was of young Private Henry Harrison, who wrote a chirpy letter home to his parents on Christmas Eve only to be killed by shrapnel the day after Boxing Day. Back home the Derby Scheme figures for Ashton were good. The number of men eligible for attesting for military service had numbered 11,200. Of these 5,093 had attested and 4,300 were in munitions work or other reserved occupations. The Queen's Electric Theatre in Ashton was showing a film called *Tattered Belgium* about the destruction of that country by the war, and this may have encouraged some to go and fight. Lord Kitchener's initial appeal for troops followed by Lord Derby's Scheme for attestation had certainly been successful in Ashton, and had other towns shown the same enthusiasm there might have been no need for compulsory conscription. But that was not the case and there were large numbers of young men who had not attested. The passing of the Compulsory Conscription Act was big news and widely debated. Men would now be forced to enlist and fight unless exempted by age, medical fitness, or they were working in a starred occupation deemed essential for the war.

The lighting in Ashton streets was to be reduced due to the threat of air attack by Zeppelins. One Ashton man swore he had heard a Zeppelin pass overhead under heavy cloud cover. He had not been able to see it but had recognised the distinctive rumble of its engines. Ashton Council, along with other local councils, discussed the prospect of Zeppelin raids, of darkening their towns and of taking extra insurance cover for corporation property and the District Infirmary. Lighting restrictions would be coming into force, which would darken all towns and villages, and there was grumbling that it would be 'back to the Dark Ages'. It was decided that in case of an air-raid attack, all borough electric lights would be lowered for three seconds and then switched off. This would be repeated three times as a warning and then all lights would be switched off for the duration of the attack. Although there was a number of air-raid attacks on Lancashire by Zeppelins, Ashton was never hit. Subsequently, this was attributed to the complete and successful blackout of the town. On their night raids the Zeppelins simply had no idea Ashton was there because there was nothing to see.

Down on the ground there were mutterings about 'Darkest Ashton' and the problems it caused. The kerbstone edges of the pavements were painted white so they were more visible to street traffic and pedestrians, and there was talk of whitening the tramway posts. Shop windows were initially blacked out an hour-and-a-half after sunset, although this restriction was later relaxed so that 'a subdued 50 candlepower light could be placed for every one and half yards of shop frontage but the windows still had to have blinds'. All lights had to be turned down or turned out at the same time. There was to be no 'time cribbing'. Every dwelling was also required to have blinds or adequate heavy curtaining.

To the annoyance of the townsfolk, youth crime and vandalism were increasing and becoming a real problem. Damage to street lamps in town had already cost £40 (approximately £1,200) to repair and there were numerous burglaries. The authorities finally decided to make an example of a gang of boys who had been breaking and entering, stealing and causing damage. There were a half-dozen of them aged from 6 to 13. Accepting that the younger ones may have been led or coerced into misdeeds, the magistrates ordered the three eldest offenders to receive six strokes of the birch each. There were suggestions that lessons in manners should be taught in schools since teachers could often exercise more authority over wayward children than their parents. Strangely, the German educational methods were rather admired by local traders and teachers. The aim of German education was subservience to the state and lack of individualism. The aim of English education was responsibilities to the empire and the formation of individual character. It was this latter aim that caused all the problems, according to many, since individualism led to radical thinking and rebellion.

Ashton Traders Association were fundraising to purchase comforts for the men in the military hospitals and grumbling bitterly that the lighting restrictions were encouraging trade to go elsewhere. As everywhere else in the locality had the same lighting restrictions, this was probably unlikely. The pubs, hit hard by the closures for selling alcoholic drinks, started to get round the problem by opening all day as before, but as cafés selling tea, coffee, meat extracts, soft drinks and mineral water. The clubs were suffering badly from the No Treating order. Ashton Council called the ban on drink 'idiotic restrictions', and said it was unnecessary and likely to encourage secret drinking at home. They embarrassed themselves and the town by protesting to the government about it and pleading for exemptions, without a mandate to do so, which attracted much criticism.

Flour and sugar prices were still rising and there seemed to be a general shortage of meat and sugar. The drive to make lump sugar a luxury was not succeeding and customers still demanded lump, crystals or granulated in equal quantities. Sugar rationing was both feared and expected for the world supply of sugar had decreased by 2,000,000 tons (one ton equals 1,016kg) as a result of the war. The price of butter and cheese had also risen as there were now no Irish supplies. There were taxes on tea, coffee and cocoa. The latter presently cost four-times what it had pre-war. There was a new tax placed on matches (both safety and ordinary) and also on all entertainments. Strangely, the tax on entertainment did not cause much fuss, perhaps because, unlike food, it was not a necessity of life. The unkindest cut of all was an Ashton chip shop which, owing to the high price of potatoes and fat, refused to sell less than a pennyworth (about 12p) of chips. Children, who had already had their sweets rationed, had also lost another treat of their 'ha'porth (about 6p) of chips in paper with lots of vinegar'.

It had been a bitterly cold winter, the coldest for a decade, with more snow and less than half the normal hours of sunshine. Easter was late and Good Friday was wet. Stamford Park and all the theatres put on good entertainments to try and lighten the mood a little. Sports fixtures went ahead, but Ashton and District Field Naturalist Society were forced to cancel their exhibition because so many members were away serving in the war. On Easter Monday, 24 April, an Easter Rising by the Irish Republicans was mounted in Dublin. Their aim was to end British rule in Ireland. Some Ashton lads got caught up in the Sinn Fein uprising but the British Army in Ireland quickly suppressed the rebellion, though it all detracted from what should have been a united front against a common enemy. Ashton had an Irish Association but the events in Ireland were overshadowed by the war, attestation and compulsory conscription. Recruitment was having a serious knock-on effect on local trades and industries, and there were numerous claims and appeals. However, few were allowed. Women could do much of the work quite efficiently although they might lack the strength for the heavier occupations of carriers, colliers and lumberjacks. Ashton and Hurst were forming a joint committee under the Naval and Military War Pensions Act, which now included women. Eight groups of attested married men had been called-up under the Military Services Act and the debate of single men versus married men rumbled on although, while it was acknowledged that married men might have more responsibilities, a number of single men also had responsibilities for parents, siblings and other family members. Compulsory conscription did not really differentiate much. Ten classes of men aged 19-29 were called-up and the appeals tribunals were kept busy. The Pelham Committee issued a list of certain occupations it considered should be exempt from call-up service:

### Agriculture
- farm labourer
- market gardening
- fruit growing
- seed raising
- making and repairing agricultural machinery
- agricultural education and organisation

### Forestry
- cutting of timber
- hauling of timber
- preparing of timber

### Shipping
- mercantile marine
- shipbuilding and ship repairing

### Transport
- railways
- canals
- docks and wharves
- cartage connected with docks and wharves

### Public utility services
- sanitary services (local authorities)
- fire brigade
- civil hospitals
- workhouses
- infirmaries
- asylums

### Red Cross and general welfare
- in camps
- in munitions factories
- in internment camps

### Cotton industry
- minders
- piecers
- twiner doublers

### Munitions
- all workers engaged in the manufacture of munitions

The local appeals tribunals dealt with a number of claims for exemption from men who either had a number of people dependent upon them and who would suffer real hardship if they enlisted, or from men running small businesses, which they would lose if they were called-up. In the end there was a total of about 800 appeals and the tribunal sittings were extended to accommodate them. Many appeals were dismissed. The tribunals were not unsympathetic but decided that everyone should have to make some kind of sacrifice for the war. Exemptions were only granted on the understanding that the individual found work in one of the exempted occupations for three days each week. Conscientious objectors were a bit harder to deal with, especially if they refused to be flexible on certain points. Most were given the choice of finding full-time employment in an exempted occupation within ten days or they would be ordered to sign-up, although they would go on non-combative duties only. Many conscientious objectors accepted this but there were still those who refused and they faced arrest and punishment. Although they were often supported by church ministers, the subject of conscientious objectors was a contentious one, especially with serving soldiers as might be expected. But tempers frayed when Mr Salthouse, a grocer from Ashton, none of whose eight sons had enlisted due to being conscientious objectors, appealed against call-

*Ashton Town Hall, c1914. (courtesy of Tameside Local Studies)*

up for any of them. Four were rejected on medical grounds but the remaining four were ordered to enlist. Mr Salthouse protested that he would not consent to this but was silenced when the tribunal chairman told him that his consent was not required and was not an issue. His sons were being called-up according to the law of the land.

No one really had the heart for May Day celebrations and the occasion was very muted; just a few gaily decorated horses as had long been the custom. The town was too focused on the call-up question and the heavy losses that the Territorials, and also the local 6th Cheshires, were suffering. The army had realised, too late, the dangers of Pals or Mates battalions in that it often meant the deaths of a number of men from just one or two streets. There were casualties too in the navy and in the air force. One Ashton air mechanic had a lucky escape when he lived to describe 'the strange sensations at a height of 9,000 feet' (around 2.75km) as his plane was shelled, although luckily not hit. Ashton folk were terribly proud of what their soldiers, sailors and airmen were doing, but families lived mainly in an agony of suspense. The daily casualty lists no longer gave battalions so identification was harder and took longer. Married men up to the age of 35 were now being called-up. They were told that they must shave off their beards, although they could retain close-shaved moustaches, the reason given being that, as Alexander the Great had discovered over 2,000 years before, the enemy could grab soldiers by their facial hair and inflict horrendous injuries upon them.

One of the major problems with calling-up married men was that it often broke up homes that had taken years of saving to put together because, with the breadwinner absent and on the pittance of army pay, those left behind could not afford to maintain a home on the meagre separation allowance. Just because there was a war on did not stop landlords putting up the rents. It was selfish and unpatriotic perhaps, but not illegal. Hundreds of houses became vacant in Ashton as families doubled-up with each other to save money and often allowances had to be paid out to soldiers' dependants without a proper address of their own. It was an administrative nightmare. Added to high rents, rising food prices were a constant problem and claims for increased allowances and financial help were common. Those on separation allowance were tested after a man wrote to the local paper stating that he could save 2s 6d (approximately £3.75) per week on a weekly wage of £1 (just under £30). A distraught lady with a child to care for and forced to live on 17s 6d (just over £26) per week responded by sending in her shopping list and asking exactly how and where she could cut down. Rent was 5/-; 12s 2d went on food, laundry, soap, coal and matches, leaving 4d for gas, clothing, tram fares and sweets.

A typical weekly shopping list for an adult and child for a week who were living on the separation allowance is given below:

| | |
|---|---|
| Bread | 1s 6½d |
| milk | 1s 6d |
| sausages | 9d |
| rabbit | 1s 6d |
| ¼lb tea | 7d |
| ½cwt coal | 8½ d |
| 4 meat faggots | 4d |
| margarine | 5d |
| sugar | 9d |
| 1lb bacon | 1s 2d |
| oats | 5d |
| beans | 1½ d |
| marmalade | 3½ d |
| 2oz cocoa | 2½ d |
| potatoes/greens | 6½ d |
| 2 packets soup | 4d |
| ½lb cheese | 6d |
| laundry | 7d |
| soap, matches | 3d |

Ashton Operative Spinners stated that wages in the cotton industry had gone up by 10 per cent while food prices had risen by 65 per cent. In mid-May the Cardroom Operatives and Spinners held a ballot and opted in favour of a 10 per cent advance on wages. They were supported by the Weavers Amalgamation and the Warpers and Winders. All agreed that unless a settlement was reached, they would all hand in their notice at the beginning of the following week. Staff were so scarce that this would force the mills to close and that could not be done. It was a hard bargaining tool.

Ashton Council chose this moment to increase their electricity tariffs. The tariffs for the Corporation Tramways and direct current users would go up by 25 per cent while those for domestic users would rise by 10 per cent. It was, unsurprisingly, not a popular move. In addition to this the borough electrical engineer and his two assistants were to receive war bonuses. Trying to think of ways to save fuel, lighting and blackouts, the government came up with a new Daylight Saving Act under the powers invested in them by the Defence of the Realm Act (DORA). It came into force on 21 May 1916. The clocks were to go forward by one hour and would remain so until around the end of September when the days started to draw in and the clocks would be put back an hour. Putting the clocks on by an hour was no problem but, unfortunately, clocks at that time had no reverse winding mechanism, so laborious instructions were issued about winding them forward eleven hours when it was time to go back an hour. The twenty-four-hour clock was not in use so all clock faces were simply numbered 1-12, which made the process and principles a little easier. British Summertime (BST) is now standard practice, but this was the first time it had ever been done. A few grumbled but it was mostly children who complained that they had to go to bed while it was still light.

Ashton Trades Association was having an active time. They campaigned vociferously on behalf of small businesses, shop owners and sole proprietors who had attested to be placed in a special reserve for home defence and sent a resolution to this effect to Lord Derby, Sir Max Aitken and the prime minister. The traders also contributed to fundraising for wounded soldiers in the local military hospitals and supported Mrs J. A. Wild of Richmond Street in Ashton in the fundraising she was organising so she could send weekly parcels of food and clothing to Ashton men held in German prisoner-of-war camps. In addition they contributed towards a motor ambulance that would be sent to France for the Red Cross. At the same time the traders helped the council to form Ashton and District League for the Blind, which was run on trade union lines and designed to prevent exploitation of blind workers.

As ever, though, it was military matters that occupied the minds of most Ashton folk. The king praised the Ashton Brigade of the Royal Artillery and the local newspaper ran a congratulatory headline 'Ashton lads are her pride'. Ashton sailors took part in a great naval victory over the Germans in a battle that took place in the North Sea. The 181st Ashton Artillery smashed through German defences in a French town. Praise and honours were heaped on the Territorials and there was a 'rousing reception and civic welcome' for Gallipoli Day held in Manchester, to which they were invited. There were further pleas for furloughs for those Territorials who had not been home for two years, and there were strongly voiced complaints that some ex-soldiers who were invalided out of the army were not receiving any pension. The pension scheme for soldiers was a shambles and, if a soldier was invalided out of the army for a reason not listed under Army Complaints, he got nothing. There was outrage in Ashton. Men had given limbs and lives and untold suffering devotion for their country and this was to be their reward. The local paper reported on a strange and mysterious happening from the Western Front in France. Several Ashton soldiers out on duty one Saturday midnight witnessed what appeared to be a sign of the cross in the sky. It lasted for about fifteen minutes before disappearing. Reason says that this phenomena was either caused by gun smoke or certain meteorological conditions, but romance says that maybe someone really was watching over them. Then, in early June, the people of Ashton were 'simply stunned' to learn of Lord Kitchener's death. He was drowned when a German U-boat torpedoed his destroyer HMS *Hampshire* off the Orkney Islands.

The Whitsuntide holidays were postponed, or rather abandoned in Ashton this year. Processions were cancelled, no bands, trips or treats were arranged, and it would be business, or work, as usual. It was almost as though the death of Lord Kitchener had caused a mass depression. The day-schools would still close and a field day was planned for the children, but otherwise church services were to be the only celebration. Then, at the last minute, the mills decided to close down from Thursday evening until Tuesday morning. This caused considerable confusion and anger, but the Ashton and District Cotton Employers Association said they were only

*Barracks Gateway, Ashton, c1918.*

following the example of other cotton manufacturing towns in Lancashire. However, cancelled holiday plans could not be resurrected and there was no time to organise any processions or entertainment. Elementary teachers were labelled 'selfish' for taking the holiday, although they doubtless needed it after teaching the ever-growing classes that were full of demanding children. The munitions workers did not join in the holidays either, but the female workers were fed up, for they felt disinclined to cook and clean after a day in the factory while their male counterparts were free after work had finished, and they had been greatly looking forward to a break. A memorial service for Lord Kitchener was held towards the end of the month but this did little to dispel the gloom.

In June the war poet Wilfred Owen finished his military training and was given a commission as second lieutenant in the Manchester Regiment. His life until that point seems to have been divided mainly between Shropshire and Birkenhead, and he was fond of books and writing poetry but wasn't known as a war poet at that stage, simply just another officer. At first he did not like the men under his command because of what he described as 'their loutish behaviour' and he dismissed them as 'expressionless lumps', but he soon changed his opinions and he learned to respect them. The Manchesters fought well side-by-side with him in France and rescued him when he was almost blown to pieces by a trench mortar. Suffering from shell-shock he was sent to hospital in Edinburgh to convalesce and it was here he met another war poet, Siegfried Sassoon. They became firm friends and Sassoon helped Owen with his poetry, his style, and his use of the language. After the war, Sassoon became responsible for promoting Owen's poetry. Both Owen and Sassoon believed in realism, in telling it how it was, not in the romantic fashion of the glory of war. Wilfred Owen was killed in action at the very end of the war, on 4 November 1918, and was awarded the Military Cross posthumously. The news of his death reached his parents on Armistice Day.

One of his most famous poems, inspired by his experiences in fighting with the Manchesters, was *Anthem for Doomed Youth*, which begins:

> *What passing-bells for these who die as cattle?*
> *Only the monstrous anger of the guns.*
> *Only the stuttering rifle's rapid rattle ...*

The Battle of the Somme, which began on 1 July, changed the face of the war. It was meant to be a turning point towards ending the war. Instead it became a turning point for loss of life and morale and of how people saw the war. General Sir Douglas Haig had taken over command of the troops after Kitchener's death. The attack and the battle were meant to last one day. Instead hostilities lasted 141 days until well into November. Many soldiers in the British Army were inexperienced, being mainly those who had responded to Kitchener's call to arms. Nevertheless, the modus operandi of sending British troops 'charging over the top' was nothing short of suicidal. Eye-witness accounts vary but what cannot be ignored is hard evidence. Certain of victory, Haig requested cameras to film the battle that took place on 1 July. The film has survived showing just what the troops faced. On that day alone over 19,000 British soldiers were killed and 38,000 were wounded. Much has been written about the Somme, both positive and negative, but, by the end, Britain suffered a total of 500,000 casualties, of whom 100,000 died, to gain just 6 miles of territory. There was very muted reporting of the battle, doubtless due to the fact that the military authorities did not want the full truth known at that point. The battle was not referred to then as the Battle of the Somme but as the Grand Attack or The Great Push. The first ten days of Haig's campaign 'cost Ashton dear in life and limb' and 'with tears of gallant pride we mourn our gallant dead' wrote the local paper. There were stories of 'Glorious Deeds of the 6th Cheshires in the Grand Attack' and '181st Artillery Brigade withstand a tear gas shell attack'. But Ashton had already given so generously of its sons at Gallipoli, and now the town was being called upon to give even more. Everyone knew someone who had lost a husband, father, brother, son. Several families lost more than one member. It was tragedy on a scale the likes of which had not been known before. There was a commemorative service held in the Parish Church on 4 August to mark the second anniversary of the war. One can only guess at what went through the minds of those who attended the service, although many must have found it hard to keep faith with a war that had killed so many and seemed so never-ending. They must have been asking themselves, 'what is it all for?' The struggle to keep calm and carry on must have been monumental and it is a testament to Ashton's spirit that, somehow, the town managed to find the strength do just that.

As so often when in shock, people focused on mundane, everyday matters. There was news of improvements in telecommunications so that now it was no longer necessary to ask for 'trunk' when making long-distance phone calls, just giving the number and being put through more quickly than before. There were concerns at Ashton lending library that borrowing figures were down due to the continuance of the war and its consequent effect on people's lives and activities. There was an ever-increasing shortage of paper and some wit suggested that folk should revert to using a slate and chalk. Shoppers were asked to bring their own paper and string, or even a basket, for their purchases. Tram drivers joined the list of exempt occupations because the authorities were finding it impossible to get women to drive the trams. A modified pay-as-you-enter system (if passengers had the correct money) had been inaugurated on the trams to save the lady conductors from dashing up and down the stairs for individual fares. Folk worried about the increasing cost of food (many shops now required a minimum spend of 4/- (about £6) before shoppers could purchase a pound (425grams) of sugar) and fuel and school materials, but fundraising work for the troops, the wounded and the prisoners-of-war was as keen as ever. There was a meeting held in Ashton Town Hall which decided to open an official prisoner-of-war fund to supplement the work being done by Mrs J. A. Hyde, and Lady Aitken was to be its president. Ashton Savings Bank was doing well and had increased its holdings for war loans, Exchequer Bonds and government stock to £2,904 10s 4d (around £86,400). Local firms and employees bought savings stamps each week, which they affixed to savings cards, and the scheme was monitored and administered by war savings committees. The Army Pensions Board was overburdened with work and there were delays in assessing cases so Ashton War Pensions Committee was appointed to deal with allowances and pensions for soldiers' wives and dependants in the town. One case involved a widow whose only son went insane at the age of 19 after being shelled and gassed. Her 5/- (approximately £7.43) per week allowance was stopped by the army as her son was no longer of any use to them. The committee could also make loans and grants in exceptional circumstances to those in difficulties. The war-induced and rapidly increasing costs of living were not, however, regarded as 'exceptional

*Richmond House Military Hospital, Ashton, c1916. (courtesy of Tameside Local Studies)*

circumstances' and any applications based on those grounds were not eligible for assistance.

There was a scare in August that foreign-made shaving brushes had been infected with anthrax. Ashton sanitary authorities were quick to react and ordered that all shaving brushes not made in Britain should be destroyed. It was too late for one local reverend gentleman. He had bought one of the infected brushes and taken it on holiday to Blackpool. He used the brush only once before throwing it away because it was too soft. On the occasion that he did use it he nicked himself shaving. A tiny cut but it was enough. A few weeks later he was dead. People were horrified and disbelieving. War or no war, it was a mean and underhand trick to play in poisoning shaving brushes with a deadly disease.

There were, however, tell-tale signs that the stress of the war and its ever-growing number of casualties, together with all the worries and privations, were taking a toll on those left at home. There were reports in the local papers of an increase in Ashton of 'unlawful wounding' and a 'deplorable increase in the use of the poker as a weapon of assault in domestic quarrels'. Pleas were made for more self-control, especially as the police had extra work to do for the military and little enough time to deal with domestic spats. The cases reported to the NSPCC were increasing as well. One hundred and eleven cases had been reported in recent months, and during the previous year 217 boys and 202 girls (of which totals fifty-seven were under 2) were affected. More attention was now focused on childcare because of 'the war's toll on the nation's manhood' and the need to replace the young men who had been killed was recognised. The birth rate for July 1916 had been the lowest for years, but the death rate amongst infants under 5 was actually greater than the deaths in the war. Decreases in income, financial worries, harsh and cramped living conditions due to the war were blamed and so was increased drinking amongst women.

After the shambles of the Whitsuntide holidays it was decided that the Wakes Week holiday would take place. Shops would close for three days from Tuesday to Thursday and the mills would close for a whole week. It was decided that the holiday was necessary to cope with the 'heavy mental strain of the war and the extra work caused by depleted manpower'. Stamford Street was 'like a deserted village'. The sole exception to taking a holiday would be the munitions workers to whom tribute was paid and there was praise for their patriotism. Munitions workers earned £5 (around £149) a week, which was a good salary for those days, but they paid a price with the toll exacted on their health. However the Wakes proved to be 'an unsettled holiday due to the war and the weather', the 'smiling faces were masks that hid care and sorrow' and there was a slump in Wakes Week weddings . Those who could afford to do so went away for the week. For the many who stayed at home there was a market and a fair but not many were in the mood for enjoying themselves and there were not even many cases of drunkenness; although some clubs evaded the No Treating order and were fined accordingly. There were 102 summonses for after-hours drinking in the clubs and seventy-eight of those had been in one club. At the back of everyone's mind was the war and the fact that the troops could have no holidays when they could leave all the carnage behind and return to Blighty for a few days. Many soldiers called Britain Blighty without understanding why, but the name came from the Hindustani word for 'home', which was 'Bilati', and which had been used by British troops serving in India during the days of the Raj.

The Armoury was to be utilised as a day room for wounded soldiers. It already had a canteen, a reading room and essentials for recreation and games. The drill hall could be used for concerts. There were still heavy casualties at the Front and the military hospitals in Ashton were full. Soldiers at the Lake Hospital were upset by a 7pm curfew which meant that those fit enough to walk could not go out in the town in the evenings to enjoy concerts or events like those in other hospitals could. The Lake Hospital, which was adjacent to the District Infirmary, was a military hospital that had to abide by military rules and the curfew remained in force.

One wounded Territorial was outraged to find himself in the paupers ward at Ashton Union Workhouse and wrote to the local paper in protest. Townsfolk felt this was no way to treat a man who had willingly given his service to his country, and he was rapidly moved to the District Infirmary. There were so many to treat and harassed doctors classified wounded soldiers by means of tying a blue cloth shape to one of their arms:

- an oblong meant fit for active service
- a triangle meant fit for garrison duty abroad
- a diamond meant fit for home service only
- a circle meant unclassified and in need of further treatment
- a square meant ready for discharge

There were now so many casualties arriving home that the Board of Guardians was making provision at the Infirmary for the care of another thirty to fifty soldiers. The District Infirmary, unlike the other hospitals, was the only hospital under the Western Command that had never received a penny for the care of wounded soldiers, and it was felt that it was now time to apply for assistance as £3,000 (approximately £89,160) was needed to arrange care and accommodation for the extra wounded soldiers. As it happened, that never became necessary as donations made from the town for the project totalled £2,817 (approximately £83,721).

In mid-September the Pavilion showed the official film of the *Battle of the Somme*, photographed by permission of the War Office during the big push in France. This was a surprising move in view of the original virtual news blackout of the battle, but it was no doubt heavily edited and designed to be used as propaganda to encourage men of fighting age to enlist voluntarily. It also focused on the initial battle on 1 July. The fact the battle was still ongoing was not emphasised. By this time there was 'a blood brotherhood and blood sisterhood in the town as most people have lost someone close to them'. Ninety-nine soldiers from forty-six houses in one Ashton district had died in battle. There were severe doubts about the film being shown and some talked of film censorship, especially for the children. However, the view that prevailed in the end was 'if soldiers have the courage to fight in it, we should have the courage to see it'.

Boys born in 1899 were invited to attest, which meant that 17-year-olds were now enlisting in the forces. A Volunteer Corps was to be formed in Ashton from conditionally exempted men. They would have to join-up for three years, wear a uniform and train at least once a week. Territorials casualties were still heavy, but there were more honours as well. An Ashton doctor, Dr Wilfred Sneath, was awarded the Military Cross for bravery in dressing wounds under heavy machine-gunfire, and another Ashton doctor, Dr A. B. Ross, wrote moving accounts of his experiences at the Front under shellfire. Five days before the commemoration service for the start of the war, five Ashton gunners, showing great gallantry and bravery, died together on the battlefield when one of their number

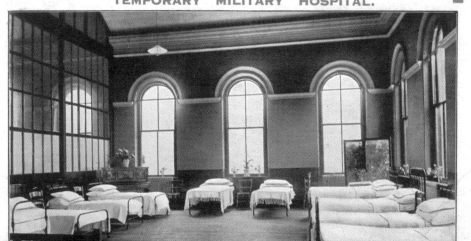

*Mechanics Institute Military Hospital, 1914. (courtesy of Tameside Local Studies)*

had fallen mortally wounded and the other four died trying to rescue him. Two Ashton soldiers were also awarded the Military Medal for assisting wounded troops. War Shrines, or Rolls of Honour, were becoming common throughout the Borough. An unexpected bonus occurred, however, in early October when thirty-four members of the 1/9th Battalion returned home for six weeks leave after spending two years away in Egypt and the Dardanelles.

Normal time returned to Ashton at the end of September when the clocks went back an hour. Lighting restrictions were to be rigidly enforced as defence against the (now very real) threat of air-raids, and also as an economy measure in the use of coal because coal output was not increasing and prices were rising. Schools would need to be commandeered as refuges for the homeless in case of Zeppelin attacks, and further advice on what to do in case of air attacks was given out. The Home Office announced that from the end of October it would prefer shops to close around 6-6.30pm, but Ashton Traders rejected those hours as being too early. The government included some restrictions, however, and insisted that shops should close by 7pm on weekdays and 9pm on Saturdays. The only exemptions were to be cafés that sold take-away food and chemists. Hairdressers and barbers would be allowed to operate until 8pm. There were several representations made about these restricted opening hours and, in the end, the government conceded that shops could remain open until 8pm on weekdays, 9pm on Saturdays, and that all cafés would now be exempt. Daylight shopping was becoming the custom and at night Ashton was taking on a rather dismal appearance. There was also a further move to restrict drinking. The country as a whole was spending more on alcohol than on shells. It was estimated that national spending on drink was costing £1million (nearly £30million) per day with half spent on the beverage itself and half on control and management, and that it was interfering with the Forces, food production, industry and munitions. Britain was condemned as 'the most backward of all the Allied countries in regards to drink'. Russia had prohibited the drinking of vodka, and the Italian Army was banned from drinking alcohol and these were just two of the examples of restraint given. It was asserted that 'no nation, not imbecile intellectually, would make alcohol a national drink'. If folk at the time could have seen into the future that might have caused a few wry smiles.

The rector of Ashton suggested a memorial chapel in the parish church to commemorate those who had fallen in battle, but this was modified to a memorial reredos, the sketch plan for which was presented at the end of November. There had recently been heavy casualties for both the Territorials and the local 6th Cheshires. Private W. Monkridge, an Ashton boxer, was awarded the Military Medal for rescuing comrades under heavy shellfire and Rifleman Albert Mellor of Ashton was awarded the Military Cross for gallantry and bravery in delivering vital messages at the Front. The Territorials were commended for 'brilliant work' but it came at a heavy cost and the need for fighting men remained acute. The government announced its intention to de-badge all unskilled and semi-skilled workers in the munitions factories so that these workers could be called-up. Age limits had recently been raised for those in exempted occupations and there were a number of tribunal appeals being heard. Parcels for prisoners-of-war and sixty extra Christmas parcels had been dispatched, the latter containing tins of soup and corned beef, Christmas puddings and Christmas cakes, knitted scarves and pairs of socks. The people of Ashton always dug deep into their pockets when it came to the troops and somehow managed to send constant gifts and parcels both abroad and to the local military hospitals at home. There was a good response to appeals for Christmas gifts to be sent to members of the 1/9th Battalion in Salonika. The Mechanics Institute and Lake Military Hospital gave many thanks for the Christmas gifts and goodies received in December. James Hamilton bequeathed £506 (just over £15,000) to the District Infirmary. No effort was spared for wounded troops. The YMCA opened the Khaki Club for convalescing soldiers' recreation. It had a reading and writing room where paper and envelopes were supplied free of charge. Games and light refreshments were also available, and it quickly became one of the most popular places in Ashton for those soldiers well enough to take advantage. Most folk seemed to accept by now that the war wasn't going to be over any time soon.

The question of lighting was still contentious, so too was that of shop opening hours. Ashton Traders sent a memo to its members which was a reprimand to those contravening the DORA restrictions by staying open and serving until 8.20pm instead of closing at 8pm. The restrictions also had an adverse effect on those selling perishable goods and many butchers were now opening on Sunday mornings, having been forced to close at 9pm instead of midnight on Saturday. Although sales and bazaars were not subject to the closing hours restrictions, there was always the problem of lights. Due to the danger of Zeppelin raids this was essential, and during an actual raid all lights were to be extinguished. Some people objected to this vociferously, but it was necessary for everyone's safety that the rules were obeyed. There were numerous accidents and there were pleas from both employers and employees for lighting restrictions to be relaxed for workers going to and from their place of work. Women and girls were especially vulnerable, not only to accidents but also to the unwanted attentions of certain men. The Home Secretary finally agreed to amend the lighting order that lights should be out by 11pm, re-lit at 5am and turned out again at 6.30am, and early closing orders were suspended for the period 14-23 December. But the usual black-out restrictions remained in force. Food prices were still rising, sugar was still a scarce commodity, and those on pensions of 12s 6d (around £18.58) were told that the separation allowance of 5/- (approximately £7.43) was not payable. In several cases, 2s 6d (about £3.72) was dispensed to try and help those unfortunate people by Ashton Old Age Pensions Committee. Ashton Savings Bank was still doing well and wartime thrift had seen its funds increased by over £26,000 (approximately £772,720).

In the week before Christmas the Ashton MP, Sir Max Aitken, was suddenly elevated to the peerage, becoming Lord Beaverbrook, so he could 'attend to Government work'. As a lord he could no longer be an MP and Sir Arthur Stanley, president of the Board of Trade, was appointed without election to be MP for Ashton. It annoyed the local Conservatives and Liberals that there had been no prior consultation, but there was general acceptance of the situation. It was difficult to wish folk a happy Christmas because of all the bereavements suffered. Some saw the festive season as a brief respite from their cares and woes, but the losses and triumphs of the war touched everyone and there was a kind of universal sympathy that crossed the class barriers with 'a deeper sense of intimacy' in these sad times. The Christmas performance of the *Messiah* at the Empire Hippodrome was a success, but the local paper dubbed the Christmas season 'a topsy turvy Christmas' because there were 'no street lights, curtailed rail services, increased rail fares, war bread [a kind of black bread which few people liked], no icing on

Christmas cakes, little turkey or meat due to prohibitive prices, great scarcity of sugar, almost no ingredients for Christmas puddings, and not so many cards or presents'. The spirit of the season was not too dampened, however, because folks at home put on a brave face, always remembering the thousands of brave lads, some of whom would never return, serving abroad, and it was determined that these serving soldiers' and sailors' sacrifices should never be forgotten. Although the 'bright hopes for peace and resolution of the war' had not been realised in 1916, Ashton people prayed that 1917 would not only hopefully be a happier year, but also the year the war ended – again.

# CHAPTER 4

# 1917

It was a dismal start to 1917. The weather was bitterly cold and there was skating in Stamford Park but most people were too busy just trying to live and keep warm. Casualty lists were still long and manpower was still short. The local paper ran an article headlined 'Mud and Water ... what our boys are experiencing at the Front ... a vivid story'. Fundraising for the troops, by means of concerts, sales, recitals and shows, was still of great importance and parcels of food and comforts were sent out regularly to troops serving abroad and to prisoners-of-war. Ashton Post Office was appealing for old razors, which could be repaired and re-sharpened at Sheffield and then sent out to the troops. The Territorials continued to acquit themselves well. Private Harry Robinson had been awarded the DCM for gallantry; so too had an Ashton miner, Alfred Roberts, for 'good work on the Somme'. Three other Territorials had won the Military Cross. A number had a lucky escape when the liner HMS *Ivernia*, in which they were travelling towards Egypt, was torpedoed. They were rescued by British destroyers, although a few of them spent three hours in the sea before rescue. All were now safely at the Mustapha Barracks near Alexandria, but for how long no one knew. Ashton Alexandra Day Committee vowed to take care of disabled soldiers who would receive comforts and a pension of 25/- (around £51.27) per week, and Ashton Trades Council met to discuss pensions and allowances for wounded and disabled soldiers.

Ashton Town Council decided to make a grant for the formation of a Volunteer Training Corps in the town. Neville Chamberlain introduced National Service, an Industrial Volunteers Scheme, which would last for the duration of the war, for all males between the ages of 18-61 who were not engaged on work of 'national importance'. They would receive 25/- (around £51.27) per week with free travel and a subsistence allowance. Clergy and doctors were to be mobilised as well and it was warned that even the women's turn would come eventually. Despite the cold and the great frost, the Queen's Theatre in Ashton was showing the film *Tanks in Action* as a means of encouragement and interest in the tactics of fighting.

There was further street lighting economy despite pleas for better lighting now that there was at least an hour's warning of enemy aircraft attack. Lamps were to be extinguished by 11pm and re-lit by 5am, but, on Sundays, although they would not be extinguished until 1am, they would not then be re-lit until Monday. It also gave the lamplighters a day off. There was a plea as well to use gas for cooking and heating as part of the wartime economy. Beer output was restricted by 50 per cent due to a reduction in the quantity of barley. Barley was required for flour and, as one newspaper put it, it was either beer or bread. Milk was costing more to produce than the price for which it was selling, due to the increase in prices of animal feeds and the shortage of labour. The steadily rising cost of milk was giving great cause for concern. Sugar prices were also rising. The substitute of saccharin was generally disliked because it 'causes a certain amount of indisposition'. Sugar was now rationed to ½lb (about a quarter of a kilo) a week and this was causing quite a bit of grief among shoppers. Foodstuffs were costing 84 per cent more than at pre-war rates. The prices of coal, electricity, train and tram fares had also risen. For those living on separation allowance it was a nightmare. Notwithstanding this, a number of landlords tried to raise rents further, using rises in the rates as their *raison d'etre* although they could not actually compel tenants to pay increased rents during the war, but many did not realise this, and a

*Lancashire Fusiliers Memorial, Wellington Barracks, Ashton, c1920.*

clearly irritated government was forced to pass yet more regulations to the effect that rents could not be increased or increments forced from the 1914 rent levels, as per the Increase of Rent and Mortgage Interest (War Restriction) Act 1915, in order to prevent profiteering from high rents during the war. In Ashton, a Tenants Defence League was formed to protect tenants from high rents and to ensure that landlords who contravened the Act were fined.

The question of allotments and cultivation of land was now being taken seriously and a scheme was outlined, along with the inevitable hints on the successful growing of potatoes. It was believed that smallholdings would promote industry and thrift as in France. There was a national call to grow potatoes and vegetables, and to keep fowl, rabbits and pigs. Clubs and committees were formed to organise matters and the government offered loans for seed potatoes and pigs, and to supply manures, plants and implements. 'A pig and a vegetable patch' became the motto, working on the principle that the pigs could be fed on any waste. Ashton covered about 1,345 acres, of which just 16½ acres were available for growing food, and Ashton Corporation vowed it would supply the seeds and loan equipment for allotments. There were initially about fifty applications for allotments but some of those applying had little horticultural experience. Samuel Turner, the superintendent of Stamford Park, undertook to write a regular column in the local paper giving hints for growing, what to grow, when to plant and how to treat the land generally. 'Plant in spring, hoe in summer, lift in autumn' was the general maxim. Everyone, including women and children, would be called upon to give some voluntary help with the work in their spare time. Women were working equally as hard and equally as effectively as men in medicine, munitions, teaching and the factories, and this also proved to be the case in agriculture, even though women often earned far less than men. The case of the suffragettes was being proved time and again and the male establishment began to accept that it was 'becoming imperative that they [women] should have a voice in future legislation'.

A War Savings Committee was formed in Ashton and £5,000 (just over £123,000) of war loan was available for distribution at 10 per cent interest of the amount taken. Ashton's contribution to the war so far totalled over £1 million (around £25 million) in terms of war loans and war savings, and funds were still coming in. There were thirty war savings associations in Ashton with over 4,000 members. Fundraising was going well. A Café Chantant and Gift Auction was held in the Town Hall and included a donkey, a sucking pig, five brer rabbits, and sugar. It raised over £500 (just over £12,300) for the local military hospitals. Comforts (knitted socks, underwear, nightshirts and scarves) were sent out to the troops each month and regular parcels continued to be posted to the prisoners-of-war. There were numerous committees to deal with all the necessary arrangements and administration and a local humourist observed that 'the English had one striking characteristic [...] that

when anything had to be done they invariably formed a committee.'
Ashton Volunteer Corps was formed with a grant of £200 (just under
£5,000) from Ashton Town Council, and looked set to be another
success alongside the Ashton Territorials and the Ashton Artillery.
The news of war casualties continued to be grim and local nurses
were honoured for their war services, including Nurse Sydney Bolt
(female despite the name) who was mentioned in despatches to the
secretary of state for war, Lord Derby, for 'rendering valuable
services'.

Chamberlain's National Service Campaign was met with caution.
Its aims, of the provision and manufacture of food and munitions,
together with nursing, driving, clerical services and back-up
facilities for the troops was laudable enough, but there were worries
about pay and conditions, promotions and position by those who
might apply. It was announced at the end of March that women were
to be sent to France for the first time to fill clerical posts, to work
as cooks, waitresses, domestic staff, and to act as clerks,
telephonists, postal workers and drivers, in order to free up the men
so they could be sent to fight at the Front. Neville Chamberlain
made a plea for another 500,000 volunteers for National Service but
got less than half that number, and of these half were already
engaged in essential work. A large body of men was needed to work
in agriculture, mines, shipbuilding and munitions to replace the
young fit men who were being taken for the army. In addition,
despite the newly formed Women's Land Army, ploughmen were
still being repatriated from the trenches to help plough for the spring
sowings of 1917, and this was causing problems. National Service
recruits were to be mainly from the 41-61 age group and would be
paid 25/- (approximately £51.27) per week. The unions were furious
about the scheme, seeing it simply as tied labour, while the
employers used it as a threat against anyone who was a
troublemaker. Until now Ashton had a good war record and had
been quick to respond to initiatives, but perhaps this was just a step
too far. There was a muted response to the National Service
Campaign and there was apathy towards working the allotments,

joining the Volunteer Training Corps and war savings schemes. Easter passed with little joy. Rail services were curtailed, fares had increased, there was none of the usual pageantry or fun usually associated with the Easter break.

A number of important events now occurred that would affect the progress of the war. Russia was an important ally of Britain and France in the Great War, but the tsar, Nicholas II, a cousin of George V, had been forced to abdicate in mid-March following the February Revolution. The severe losses of the Imperial Army in the Great War (almost 3,500,000 men by the end of the war) and the incompetence of those in command finally turned public opinion in Russia against the tsar, who was seen as being mainly responsible for the economic and military collapse of the country. Although he and his family were not executed until July 1918, his abdication sent shockwaves throughout Europe and altered Russia's contribution to the war. In early March the British captured Baghdad and ten days later they succeeded in capturing much of Mesopotamia. However, they failed to capture the city of Gaza during the First Battle of Gaza on 29 March and had another go with the Second Battle of Gaza on 19 April, but the Ottoman defences held. Then a week later, in early April, America finally entered the war with the avowed intention of 'securing government of the people by the people for the people'.

These developments seemed to jolt Ashton out of its apathy. There was a series of meetings and a renewed drive for the National Service Campaign. A request was made for all Ashton trades people to join the Volunteer Defence Corps. All the allotments were now taken up and local folk, including schoolchildren, were working hard growing potatoes and vegetables. Tips were given in the newspaper on how to grow peas, beans, onions and leeks. It was clearly obvious that, despite pleas to the contrary, selfishness and hoarding of food, as well as shortages, were occurring, and that as food stocks were alarmingly low there had to be some sort of food control or even food rationing. This was welcomed by a number of people. Sugar was very scarce and everyone was rationed to ½lb (about ¼kilo) per week. Flour, tea and bread were also in short supply. A new loaf was introduced which included rice, barley, maize, semolina, oats, rye or beans. These additions made the bread darker and more satisfying, although it was of less nutritional value. Coal was rationed and sweets were prohibited. Ashton Food Economy Committee asked local domestic science teachers to give classes in simple and economic home cooking. Ashton War Savings Committee also took up the cry of economising on food consumption. Gluttony, they said, should be abhorred. Those who were better off should buy dearer cuts of meat and leave cheaper cuts for those with less money. There was a great deal of condemnation of unpatriotic speculators and profiteers, who bought and hoarded potatoes, beans and dry goods, to force up the prices. Andrew Bonar Law announced that Britain 'may have to suffer hardships unknown so far', and self-rationing of food was advocated. In May the king issued a proclamation, which was read out by the mayor on the steps of Ashton Town Hall and asked the people:

> [...] to reduce the consumption of bread in their respective families by at least one fourth of the quantity consumed in ordinary times [...] and to abstain from the use of flour in pastry [...]

It was advised that folk should limit themselves to one large slice of bread per day and to reduce the cakes, biscuits and tarts that they either bought or baked at home. The Ladies Health Society suggested a government grant for milk to help infants because the high cost might mean that many children were not getting enough.

Ashton had a problem with its young children in that the mortality rate for the under-5s was almost the highest in the country at 247 per thousand, which later rose to 346 per thousand. This meant that initially a quarter and subsequently a third of children in the town were dying before their 5th birthday, and even if they did survive there was then the problem of the white scourge (tuberculosis, or consumption, as it was better known) to be faced.

The high infant mortality rate was said to be due to poverty, working mothers and drink. But in fact Dr Crawshaw, an eminent local doctor, shifted the blame from the shoulders of the mothers to those of the civic authorities. Ashton was full of bad, cramped and insanitary housing that had closets (toilets) right outside the back door. The small and mean dwellings had been built during the first half of the nineteenth century to accommodate the mill workers at a time when there were few, if any, building regulations. The council had done little or nothing about these conditions, partly, but not wholly, due to the war. Farms that supplied milk were not regulated. They were dirty, there was dirty handling of the milk and storage of milk was often inadequate, again partly due to the war. The lack of health visitors, which *was* due to the war, was also responsible for maternal ignorance of basic hygiene procedures. Dr Crawshaw was ridiculed by Ashton Health Committee, but he stuck to his principles and eventually it was admitted that there should be some sort of proper housing scheme for Ashton, although this couldn't be considered until the war was over. Finally, a committee for a housing scheme was set up to look into the whole problem, decide how many houses needed to be demolished and initiate a programme for rebuilding new homes, which would also provide employment for returning soldiers.

Whitsuntide was 'fettered', with no pageants, no processions (except that of Whit Friday), no treats, no public meals (due to food restrictions) and very few bands (with the players away at the Front). But June began on a more cheerful note for Ashton. The town had an active suffragette association that had put most of its work on hold while its members helped in the war effort, but which never ceased to make the point that women could do the work men did just as efficiently and effectively. By summer 1917, the government had realised what a debt of gratitude was owed to the women of England for 'keeping the home fires burning', doing many of the jobs previously done by men, and so much more besides, while the men were away fighting. In fact, the chief inspector of factories and workshops in 1916 had admitted 'the great adaptability of women

*Munitions factory explosion, Ashton, June 1917. (courtesy of Tameside Local Studies)*

in substitution'. Finally, the proposed changes to the Electoral Reform Bill were to become law and women over the age of 30 were to get the vote. The property qualification, i.e. needing to be a property owner in order to vote, was also abolished. News from the Front was still grim but then something happened that brought home the full force and meaning of the war to Ashton in a literally explosive fashion.

Sylvain Dreyfus was a chemist who worked for the Hooley Hill Rubber and Chemical Company. He had trained in his profession in France, but when he was 22, he moved to England, initially to become manager of the Clayton Aniline Company, which was a major producer of textile dyes. He took British citizenship and met several noted chemists of the day including Chaim Wiezmann, who later became the first president of Israel. He also met a Swiss chemist named Lucien Gaisman with whom he worked in the dye business before setting up their own company, the Hooley Hill Rubber and Chemical Company, in 1914. The chemical section of this new company was based in West Street Mill, a former cotton mill, on William Street in Ashton. The War Office had a chronic shortage of ammunition early on in the war and, like many other similar firms, the Hooley Hill Rubber and Chemical Company were awarded a contract to produce TNT (Trinitrotoluene) for the Ministry of Munitions. Initially, 5 tons a week was to be produced, but this was soon increased to 10 tons. TNT is manufactured from a mixture of nitric and sulphuric acids to which toluene (a side product from the manufacture of gas) is added. TNT is stable as an explosive, although very inflammable and very toxic. Munitions workers who produced it often suffered toxic jaundice, becoming known as 'canaries' due to their yellow complexion. Mr Dreyfus instigated a new production method for the final stages, the details of which were known only to himself but which involved the use of nitric acid only instead of nitric and sulphuric acids mixed. This speeded up the process and reduced the use of acids and the costs, but made the whole mixture much more unstable.

In the late afternoon of Wednesday 13 June Dreyfus was working with a colleague, Nathan Daniels, also a chemist, in the nitrating house where toluene was added to the acid when nitric acid fumes began to leak from one of the nitration tanks. This meant the mixture became unstable. Dreyfus instructed one of his workmen, Isaac Johnson, to stop the flow of acid and the stirrer (which mixed the acid and the toluene). However, the instability reaction did not subside and the acid boiled over, releasing hot acid onto the wooden flooring, which instantly caught fire. Frank Slater, another chemist, attempted to open the cock on a nearby dryer that held a ton of explosive, but even the asbestos lagging of the dryer was already on fire. The factory fire hoses were immediately utilised, police were called and the fire brigade was summoned. Two minutes later 5 tons of TNT exploded with considerable and amazing force. The mill that had housed the munitions factory was completely destroyed. Two craters, 95 ft x 36ft x 5ft deep, remained where the packed drums of TNT had once stood. The large waste acid burners were thrown 50 yards into Ashton Canal. Two nearby Ashton gasometers, containing 850,000 cubic feet of gas, collapsed and the flames shot half a mile into the air. A hundred houses were destroyed. Victoria Street Day School, a number of buildings and the sewage works were badly damaged, and windows were shattered in several streets. Bridge End Mill caught fire in the aftermath of the explosion and collapsed, killing three more people. Claytons Corn Mill and the Forage Mill also caught fire. Knotts Mill, Tudor Mill and Junction Mill lost nearly all their windows. The noise of the explosion could be heard over 20 miles away. Portland Place Ward, the district that was worst affected, had 2,000 homes squeezed into just 179 acres. The destruction and damage to homes simply added to Ashton's problem of insufficient suitable dwelling houses. Forty-six people in total were killed, 120 injured were in hospital, and 300 to 400 suffered minor injuries. The burn and blast injuries were beyond appalling and flying glass had also inflicted some terrible wounds. The body of Sylvain Dreyfus was

*Mass funeral after munitions explosion, Ashton, June 1917. (courtesy of Tameside Local Studies)*

found by the factory gates lying in two pieces and recognisable only by labels sewn into his clothing.

The king and queen immediately sent a telegram expressing regret and sending condolences to the people of Ashton. So too did the minister for munitions, Dr Christopher Addison, on behalf of the government. When the news reached them there were sympathies from the men at the Front and those from Ashton who had emigrated to Canada. Ashton Town Council at once established three sub-committees: one to organise burials of those killed; one to organise feeding those who had lost everything; and one to deal with problems of housing the homeless. Lord Beaverbrook gave £500 (nearly £25,000). The mayor started a Distress Fund, which had reached £7,500 (approximately £318,800) by the end of June and would ultimately reach more than £10,000 (around £489,000). George Formby, the renowned singer and comedian, who had close connections with Ashton, gave a performance at the Theatre Royal in Ashton to raise funds for the victims. The inquests were held on Friday, 15 June and a public funeral for many of the victims took place on Sunday, 17 June. A local lady named Lilian Veson wrote a poem for the Ashton newspaper to commemorate the occasion, which included the very appropriate lines:

[A] strange dark shadow crept among them [...]
Death's dark angel, passing swiftly, claimed her own.

A quarter of a million people lined the funeral procession route to show their respect. A sour note was introduced when pickpockets came into the town and stole from those along the route who were paying their respects. The ministry of munitions agreed that it would 'deal with and pay all reasonable claims [...] for personal injury and damage to workmen's dwellings and other small property', although it declined to pay Ashton weavers for loss of employment caused by the explosion. Repairs to properties damaged in the explosion were given priority and the Ashton Mutual Plate Glass Insurance Company paid to replace 12,000 square feet of glass. There would be a public enquiry in due course, but it would take Ashton a long time to recover.

A national food controller was appointed and a set of new food regulations was laid down. Later, a food control committee was appointed in Ashton that had to deal with adherence to the new regulations, supply, distribution and fair prices:

- output of beer limited to a third of the output in the period 1 April 1915 – 31st March 1916
- the manufacture and sale of malt was prohibited, except under licence
- barley, oats and maize were to be used only as seed, human or animal food
- imported beans, peas and lentils were taken over by the Ministry of Food
- bread was not to be sold until it had been made for twelve hours
- loaves allowed were tin, one piece, oven bottom, pan Coburg and twin sister brick
- rolls had to weigh not less than 1oz and not more than 2oz
- no currants, sultanas or sugar in bread and no milk-bread allowed
- all bread to be sold by weight and all loaves must weigh 1lb or an even number of pounds
- no wheat, rye, rice, tapioca, sago or arrowroot to be used except as human food
- fancy cakes, muffins and crumpets were prohibited
- 15 per cent sugar was allowed in cakes and biscuits, but only 10 per cent in scones
- Food Control to oversee all imported cheese
- no hoarding
- feeding stuffs for horses rationed
- maximum wholesale price of milk was to be 6½d (approximately 66p) per gallon (nearly 4 litres); retail 3½d (about 36p) per quart (just under 1 litre)

- meat sales subject to a number of regulations
- publicly sold meals also subject to various regulations
- sugar allowed per person reduced to 25 per cent of 1915 supply
- tea and coffee to be sold by net weight

After the tragedy of the Somme and the bombardment of London by heavy duty German Gotha G.IV planes, as well as the unending bitter fighting, George V was faced with a difficult and painful decision. In the wake of his cousin, Tsar Nicholas II, abdicating from the Russian throne as a result of the February Revolution, which had followed the assassination of Rasputin at the end of December in 1916, the king was also facing the embarrassing prospect of continuing to fight another of his cousins, Kaiser Wilhelm, with whom he privately got on rather well. Anti-German feeling was running extremely high in Britain and it was felt that it was just too much to ask the British people to follow and fight for a king of German descent and bearing the very German name of Saxe-Coburg-Gotha. George V couldn't help his lineage but he could make a very public gesture of renouncing his German connections. On 17 July 1917, he issued a royal proclamation:

> Now, therefore, We, out of Our Royal Will and Authority, do hereby declare and announce that as from the date of this Our Royal Proclamation, Our House and Family shall be styled and known as the House and Family of Windsor, and that all the descendants in the male line of Our said Grandmother, Queen Victoria, who are subjects of this realm [...] shall bear the said Name of Windsor.

There were still grim lists of war casualties being posted in Ashton. 'Heavy toll of Ashton and Dukinfield Soldiers' read one newspaper headline. The Brearly family had now lost both sons to the war and were not alone in losing more than one member of their family. There were four brothers in the Hurst family who had joined-up. One had been killed, one was missing and two were wounded.

Second-Lieutenant Tom Harling was wounded three times, gassed once, and finally killed in action in France. His brother, Private George Harling, had been killed at Gallipoli. Private Tom Robinson was killed by a shell in France while his brother, Private Sam Robinson, was killed in the Dardanelles. Two Ashton doctors, Dr A.B. Ross and Dr Wifred Sneath, were killed in Flanders. One hundred years on it is still heartbreaking to look at all the photographs of the fresh, eager, good-looking young faces in the newspaper knowing that their destiny was a brutal death and, for the lucky ones, 'burial in a far corner of some distant land'. The Territorials were doing 'brilliant work' and Ashton soldiers continued to be awarded medals for gallantry and bravery. Sergeant Blades won the Military Medal for 'conspicuous bravery during a German gas attack' and was awarded an extra bar to this medal 'for bravery near Arras on Easter Monday'. Reverend A.D. Johnson was awarded the Military Cross 'for working day and night to assist the wounded in Palestine' and Second-Lieutenant Cyril Whitehead was awarded the Military Cross for 'bravery in a raid on German trenches when wounded by a German bomb'. Regimental Sergeant Major J.W. Peagram of the 2/9th Battalion was awarded the DCM for 'gallantry in No Man's Land' and Sergeant-Major T. Whittam also received the DCM for 'gallantry in the field'. Ashton District Infirmary had built a new ward block on Darnton Road with twenty-eight extra beds for treating wounded soldiers, but there was already a waiting list of at least a hundred. The cost of building this new ward block was £4,000 (approximately £98,440), of which £3,500 (approximately £78,830) had already been subscribed by Ashton folk. The Ashton mayor and the town council also spearheaded appeals and fundraising events to help support the East Lancashire Disabled Soldiers and Sailors Homes. A service was held in the parish church to mark the third anniversary of the war, but a planned service to be held in front of the Town Hall the following day had to be cancelled on direct orders from the War Office.

The traditional Wakes Week was overshadowed by both the toll the war was taking on the town and the aftermath of the terrible explosion in June. The weather was uncertain, increased rail fares meant short day trips rather than holidays away, and there was another slump in Wakes weddings. A Wakes fair was held on the Tuesday and there were various events in Stamford Park. The Theatre Royal put on the aptly named *Hindle Wakes*. A couple of weeks later Ashton and District Allotment Holders Association held their first show at the Armoury, which was well received and there was, for the moment, a surplus of fresh fruit and vegetables. Ashton Savings Bank seemed to be doing well and now had funds of over £700,000 (approximately £17,227,000). Meanwhile, there was much discontent. Ashton spinners were having a hard time due to stoppages and a reduction in imports of cotton, although the Cotton Control Scheme did its best to minimise the effects. All wage demands were refused. The carters and tram workers wanted wage rises, so too did the teachers, although unlike the former two the latter had not so far had any pay rises or war bonuses. Municipal workers also asked for pay rises, although Ashton rates had increased by 10¾d in the pound due to the effects of the war. There was 'a famine' of decent houses, exacerbated by those destroyed or damaged in the June explosion, and a number of workers now had to live outside the town. Coal was rationed and so too, in Ashton, was gas at times of high demand because, as a result of the collapse of the gasometers in the June explosion, five sixths of the storage capacity had been lost, and normal capacity would not be resumed until at least the end of November. 'Dark Ashton' was described as 'disgraceful and dangerous' and there were continual pleas for more lighting. Milk was 7d (approximately 72p) a quart (just under a litre) in Ashton and cheaper elsewhere. Tea, butter, bacon, margarine and flour were in short supply. The slowness of action over the question of food shortages and rising prices, particularly those of bread and sugar, was causing unrest, and it was eventually decided by the government that there should be a sugar card permit scheme. Shoppers would have to get a form from the post office, register, and when they received their card, deposit it with a shopkeeper of their choice. Eight million cards were issued until the government

*Ashton munitions explosion, June 1917. (courtesy of Tameside Local Studies)*

realised that the total number of applications for sugar card permits exceeded the total population by several million and withdrew the scheme. There were serious concerns voiced by many over gross inequalities in food distribution and it was considered that compulsory food rationing was necessary. Finally, it was announced that in the New Year food cards would be distributed on which weekly supplies of sugar, tea, butter, bacon, flour, jam, syrup, tinned milk and matches would be marked for each person. Folk would deposit these with a designated shopkeeper of their choice and then collect their rations on a weekly basis. Communal kitchens for cooking were also proposed in order to conserve food and fuel, but this idea was not popular.

The dark month of December was more than usually sombre. Despairing questions were now being asked about what exactly was going to happen on the Western Front as the war dragged on. There was a serious loss of confidence in the government by ordinary people who felt there was a constant belittling of all the sacrifices being made and that the country had lost its way. Folk also felt there was far too much profiteering going on. Morale was not what it was in 1914. Folk had lost sight of the purpose of the war and needed reassurance that the troops were still fighting for the original cause to establish right over might and the defeat of Germany. Casualty lists continued to make grim reading and the death of Ashton JP, Abraham Park, who had 'dominated religious, social and moral life in Ashton for fifty years', threw the town into mourning yet again. After that came the news that the former Ashton MP, Sir Max Aitken, now Lord Beaverbrook, had suffered a complete breakdown owing to exhaustion from war work. Then Ashton was informed that it was not meeting its weekly subscription to war bonds – £22,500 (approximately £553,725) for a population of just over 45,000. Each man, woman and child should contribute another 10/- (about £12.30). 'Merry Christmas' seemed to be the 'essence of irony', for there was nothing to be particularly merry about and much of the usual Christmas spirit was lacking. More street lamps were ordered to be lit over the Christmas period and early closing hours were suspended from 15-24 December for unrestricted shopping, but most had neither the money nor the heart for it. Even the District Infirmary was in £6,000 (approximately £147,660) debt, owing to the high costs of food, drugs and surgical equipment. The choice of the Theatre Royal pantomime was *Mother Goose*, a character who also had difficulty making ends meet. Fewer cards were sent although there were more parcels than usual. The soldiers and sailors overseas could never be forgotten. Tram workers, miffed at being denied their latest wage demand, refused to work over Christmas so there were no trams on Christmas Day. Although the town looked pretty with its covering of snow and decorated shop windows, there were no preparations for Christmas fun and parties and Christmas feasting was totally out of the question. No extra meat was sold over the Christmas period and there were long queues at the grocers' shops. According to the local paper 'bad will was more rampant than at any known period of history'.

# CHAPTER 5

# 1918

'Watchnight' services (an innovation by John Wesley) were held in the churches and chapels of Ashton on New Year's Eve when the thoughts of everyone who attended must have been with their loved ones fighting on the front line for their families, their country and freedom. The king issued a royal proclamation that there should be a day of prayer on the first Sunday in January for all those involved in the war effort, both at home and abroad, and a fervent hope that this *really would be* the last year of the war. It was not a good time. Many were grieving, depressed or dispirited and, in a number of cases, hungry. There was even scarce food for the horses and pigs. Although 1,200 people were now working allotments and growing as much as they could, Ashton was regarded locally as 'laggard' for not having enough allotments being taken up and worked. Part of the reason was that existing allotment holders were unhappy with their government tenancy agreements. However, by the time of their second annual show in September, the allotment holders had redeemed themselves. All the talk was of food rationing. Local food committees were trying to shorten what seemed to be never-ending queues at grocers, butchers and dairies by arranging a scheme for the sale of margarine, which was in short supply, and organising a priority scheme for milk supplies. There was a big demand for sterilised milk and, in order to cope with this, the Milk Sterilisation Committee started to sell it in evaporated, dried and liquid forms.

Tea was also in short supply and butter was quite scarce and costing 2s 6d (about £2.52) per pound (just under half a kilo). The meat supply was half of what it had been just three months before in October 1917. Ashton folk woke up one day to find drovers bringing 100 cattle into town, but most were not destined for Ashton. A local food rationing scheme was formulated for the town with cards for tea, butter and margarine. The Ministry of Food had already sent out a memorandum outlining the aims of proposed food rationing, but Ashton had problems that needed to be solved more immediately. Margarine was to be distributed by ticket and local butchers decided not to supply meat for social functions and gatherings. No mutton or rabbits were on sale, and only a small amount of fish and fowl. The supply of English-grown onions had run out. Although foreign varieties were available, they were more expensive. However, despite the ticket system of supply-instigation, people still insisted on queuing up for their margarine and milk supplies.

The Ministry of Food, under the leadership of Lord Rhondda, a survivor of the *Lusitania* and Minister of Food Control, finally decided that food rationing really was unavoidable and issued forms to be filled in by every household in the land, of which there were 10,500 in Ashton. Every customer had to register with one shop to purchase certain foodstuffs and, once registered, could not go elsewhere for them. No shopkeeper was required to register more customers than they could properly handle. Supplies would be distributed to the shopkeepers in proportion to the number of customers they had and each shopkeeper was required to divide all weekly supplies proportionately among those registered. Initially margarine, butter, bacon and meat would be rationed in addition to sugar, which had been rationed for some time. But there were delays in issuing the food coupons and organising equitable distribution which was irritating to everyone and caused much angst among workers. A consumers committee was formed with workers, Trade Council and Co-operative Society representatives as members. The Co-operative Society had already been complaining of unfair food

*Stamford Street, Ashton, c1920.*

distributions. In mid-February Lord Rhondda ordered a voluntary surrender of hoarded food, but this met with only muted success. A milk priority scheme was initiated and, in accordance with Lord Rhondda's directives, local bakers discussed how they could utilise existing machinery to use potato flour for making bread, using perhaps just a fraction of wheat flour. Lord Rhondda also designated Wednesdays and Fridays as 'meatless days for the provinces' when no meat could be served in public eating establishments. In order to conserve fuel, the idea of communal kitchens was introduced where folk could get cheap, nourishing meals at little cost, and it was hoped that many would use these at least once a day instead of using fuel to cook at home. In Ashton this idea was taken up, although with caution, and a communal kitchen, called the Borough Food Depot, opened on 11 March with a canteen capacity of 1,000 to 1,200 meals a day. An average meal would cost 5d (approximately 43p) and the Ashton caterers who were to run the place told 'make an unpleasant necessity as attractive as possible'.

Food rationing officially began in Ashton on 21 March, the same day as its neighbouring townships and the nearby town of Glossop.

Application forms had been given to shopkeepers in each local community and, when completed and approved, a certificate was issued allowing the shopkeeper to sell rationed foodstuffs. The rule was simple: no certificate, no rationed food for sale. Customers also received food distribution cards with two counterfoils: one for tea, butter and margarine; the second for other rationed goods. They were required to register with the shopkeepers allotted to them and the shopkeepers kept the counterfoils so that folk could not use them elsewhere as well, as had been a common practice. All shopkeepers had to make returns of registered customers. There was some grumbling but money could no longer talk and everyone was now getting at least some foodstuffs from all categories. Subsequently, a number of men doing heavy work were given supplementary meat rations but women, doing exactly the same work, were denied these rations, causing festering resentment, and by May the practice was discontinued. In that same month, tripe and brawn, long popular in the northern millscapes, were rationed as well. Tripe, the stomach lining of a sheep or cow and eaten with onions, is a dish that has declined dramatically in popularity. So too has brawn, a dish made of cooked pressed meat from the head of a pig. Housewives were advised to bottle as much fruit as possible and, also in May, numbers of applications for extra sugar were made so that fruit could be preserved and some jam made. This was agreed on the basis that the products made would be shared, but a considerable number refused to do this. Eggs were not rationed at this point but if they were pickled, the number had to be reported to the local food committee. There were numerous complaints about the iniquities of food rationing in the *Ashton Reporter* and, in particular, about the declining quality of meat. Six hundred locomotives had been sent, along with 200 miles of railway line that had been taken up, and 170,000 fit railway workers, to the Western Front to ensure speedy and prompt deliveries to the Front. This had an effect on moving freight and cattle at home and was partially responsible for a shortage of fresh meat and the introduction of frozen meat supplies, which were treated with great suspicion by many. The local paper ran an editorial headed 'rashers and rations', beefing about a lack of bacon and other cuts of meat. However, infant mortality was much reduced by food rationing and, ultimately, although the folk of Ashton did not know this at the time, food rationing would eradicate the diseases of poverty such as rickets and malnutrition. Ironically, 100 years on, rickets has made a re-appearance and malnutrition is glaringly obvious in the current obesity and diabetic epidemics, although today the main causes are ignorance, lack of domestic skills and a certain amount of laziness.

One group of people did at least get a Christmas lunch to remember. The troops at the Front dined on turkey, plum pudding and champagne. No one begrudged them that tiny luxury and, for some, it would be their last luxury. In late January, the king awarded six medals to local citizens for great courage shown in the immediate aftermath of the dreadful explosion at the Ashton munitions factory in June 1917. Many victims were still suffering and some would never fully recover. In February, Sergeant Richard May of Ashton became the youngest sergeant to be awarded the DCM, which he won for 'daring and coolness on the Cambrai Front'. The following month, Major T.E. Howorth, also from Ashton, was awarded the Croix de Guerre by Belgium for 'bravery on the battlefield'. Private A. Adams, another Ashton man, won the DCM for 'conspicuous gallantry and devotion to duty as a stretcher bearer'. Rifleman T. Whittam was awarded the DSM for saving the lives of three of his comrades, and Private Joseph Hibbert, a former New Cross miner, won the DSM for 'gallantry conduct during night attacks'. There was no doubting that the local soldiers were a brave and valiant bunch who had fought well, but their heroism brought heavy casualties and growing lists of killed and injured soldiers still continued to arrive. Ashton and District Infirmary reported their 'busiest period in the history of the institution', although they were now receiving more income from donations and fundraising events, if not yet enough to clear their debts. There were reports that the Germans were not treating English prisoners-of-war well and that many were not receiving the parcels of food and comforts sent out to them on a weekly basis, which provoked a good deal of fury. Fundraising for the prisoners-of-war went on constantly, for it was costing up to £100 a week to feed and clothe them. Concerts, cricket matches, a performance of *Elijah* by the local operatic society, an American tea, and a boxing carnival in the Armoury, were held to ensure that weekly consignments of food and comforts were posted out to the prisoners. Horses and petrol were urgently required for army transport and the call went out to 'spare a horse or save two gallons of petrol', which initiated various fuel economy measures. In addition, Ashton was called upon to contribute £100,000 (£2,019,000) to pay for a new submarine. If it was to do with the war nothing was ever too much trouble for the town and the amazing sum of £172,701 (around £3,486,833) was raised in 'a businessman's week'. Ashton Savings Bank funds totalled £775,000 (approximately £15,647,250), which was excellent for wartime investment. The war was taking a terrible toll on Ashton and the local paper lamented all the 'gallant men who died to stop the German onslaught'. Something had changed, however. Advances were being made and victories were being won and there seemed to be a growing optimism and a conviction that the end of the war finally was in sight, and the 'good fighting spirit of the British' was remarked upon in several quarters.

Encouraged by this news, perhaps, the government announced that parliamentary elections would take place in October, although this was later postponed until 14 December, mainly because differences in party politics had been put aside for the duration of the war and folk did not see the necessity for being side-tracked from focusing on the war by political issues. In any case, there were large numbers of voters absent serving abroad, some 6,000 or 7,000 in the case of Ashton. Electoral registration forms arrived in each household for completion and return. The numbers on the electoral registers had doubled and 8,642 more voters were registered than previously, 6,000 of them women. Maternity and Child Welfare Acts were passed that enabled grants to be made available for lying-in homes, home helps, food for mothers and infants, hospital treatment

*Ashton Baths, where folk could both swim and bathe, as they were in 1914. (courtesy of Tameside Local Studies)*

for infants, and homes for children of widowed mothers, etc. This, the government believed, would attract support from the female vote. Thus emboldened, and realising that a new generation of skilled and educated youngsters would be needed to replace those who had died on the battlefield, the government also passed a new Education Bill. The employment of children under the age of 12 was now forbidden and the compulsory school-leaving age was raised to 14. School fees for ordinary primary and secondary schools were abolished and provision was made for nursery schools, playing fields, game centres, school baths, school camps, medical inspections and physical and social training. It was revolutionary and met with howls of protest from the cotton trade, who employed youngsters because their wages were cheap and, as they were smaller than adults, they could clean under and around machinery without it having to be stopped. The government held firm, however. The war had changed everything and now 'a brave new world' had to be faced.

There had been concern for much of the war about the conditions to which soldiers and sailors would return – a lack of opportunity, jobs and decent accommodation. There was already a shortage of housing of any description in Ashton, which had been further exacerbated by the loss of 100 houses in the munitions factory explosion of June 1917. Besides, Ashton had had the third highest adult death rate in Lancashire and the fifth highest child mortality rate over the last ten-year period, which was due in no small measure to inadequate and insanitary housing. It was therefore decided that financial assistance for approved building schemes for workers' housing would be forthcoming and it was proposed to purchase land for building 1,000 new homes. The recommendations were that there should be no more than twelve houses per acre and no more than eight per row, and that each dwelling should have a living room, kitchen/scullery, three bedrooms and 'the necessary conveniences'. Cellars were deemed undesirable. There should be a small front garden, a paved backyard, front and back access, and room for ginnels (alleys) between the rows for refuse collection and coal deliveries, which would put an end to the old back-to-back housing favoured by mill-owners for their workers on grounds of space and economy. Furthermore, the houses should remain habitable for at least sixty years. The construction work would also provide employment for numbers of returning soldiers. Socialism was growing in Ashton and the Labour Party now formed in the town was to affiliate with the Trades Council. Both the Conservatives and Liberals had done little over the years to improve the lot of the working man or woman, although the 'Labour element' had usually voted for Liberal Party candidates. The vicar of St John's Church, Reverend R.W. Cummings, a vocal and much criticised Socialist churchman, was shocked and appalled by some of the houses in Ashton in which people were forced to live as a result of the 'housing famine' in the town. 'The Englishman's home is his castle,' he thundered, 'but in Ashton his castle can be just two squalid leaking rooms in one of which a family of seven has to sleep.'

Ashton Weavers paid out £5,000 (£212,500) in unemployment pay in just six consecutive weeks and Ashton spinners reported unemployment running at 50 per cent as it was in much of the cotton industry. A thousand card-room employees in Ashton were affected by stoppages. However, this did not stop cotton operatives putting in for a 30 per cent wage rise. Conscious that returning soldiers might have little hope of finding employment in the cotton trade, classes were started in boot and shoemaking/repairing for disabled soldiers and sailors. It was ironic that, at the same time, tram workers were demanding another wage rise. The teachers hadn't had a pay rise since the war began and were becoming increasingly restless. The police and municipal workers had received pay rises, stone masons received a war bonus of 12/- (approximately £12.11) per week, and local committees were formed to organise part-time labour for National Service work. Workers in the cotton trade were allowed to help with haymaking while on stoppages without affecting their rights. Youngsters were to collect waste paper and help out on the allotments. In April the Budget surprised everyone by taxing luxury trades, mostly jewellers and costumiers, as well as the usual taxes on tobacco and beer. This prompted complaints that craftsmen making good quality stuff would be badly affected and that shelves would be filled with 'worthless and shoddy tat'. Easter rail services were curtailed again, and so were Whit Week excursions because no 'frivolous use' of fuel was allowed, but it was decided to allow the Whit Friday Sunday School processions to take place. Sadly, the flowerbeds in Stamford Park had been vandalised and those who enjoyed the park gardens during the brief holiday were dismayed by the damage caused. Farmers and the now increasing numbers of allotment holders were harassed by a plague of caterpillars (a variety of the antler head moth) that threatened all crops. Birds, their normal predators, had been decimated for human consumption. Trenches were dug and fires lit in attempts to ward off or destroy the pests, but much damage was done to crops.

In June there was an outbreak of Flanders flu, or Spanish flu as it became known. The local medical officer of health denied it was an epidemic and 'although highly infectious and virulent' it was 'more inconvenient than dangerous'. There were only a 'few isolated cases' in Ashton and it was sufficient to take the usual precautions. Keep the house or school clean, send children out into the fresh air, and ensure there was plenty of ventilation. Anyone who was ill should go to bed, take an 'aperient' (medicine to relieve constipation) and live on a diet of 'hot slops'. A couple of weeks later the medical officer of health admitted it was 'the real thing', but he considered a good heavy downpour would stop the spread of the epidemic. The weather obliged and by the end of July the epidemic was abating in Ashton, although there had been twenty-four deaths, mostly from pneumonia,which had followed on from the flu. It was perhaps this outbreak that decided those who could afford it to take a holiday during Wakes Week. Special trains were laid on for Southport and Blackpool, a sign that the authorities too recognised it was necessary to get away if one could. Two thousand people packed their cases, took their ration books, and headed to Charlestown Station, leaving Ashton behind for a week. The baths closed, the post office closed for three days, the shops closed for the Tuesday, Wednesday and Thursday of Wakes Week, although the usual Wakes Fair was held on the Tuesday. The mood was lighter this year and that was due to the fact that there was a sense of excitement and expectancy in the air, but that was because the final push of the war, the Hundred Days Offensive, had begun. It was the beginning of the end of the war.

Some men in the 35-45 age group were offered special privileges if they would undertake work on the canals, but the new Military Services Act was causing real hardship to traders by calling-up men aged 41-51. It caused severe staff shortages and, in the case of one-man businesses, it was a serious problem. Folk tried to protect one-man businesses as best they could if the owner was away, but there were limits. Some businesses had to be sold and a few of these were bought up by foreign nationals. Ashton Traders were furious.

They did not want this and most of them believed that either foreign citizens should be made to do work of national importance or they should be deported. It was harsh, but these were harsh times. All traders aged 41-46 had to have fitness medicals and there was a call for 15,000 men to transfer from the Volunteer Corps to the home services. The volunteers were now forming the company of 1st VB Manchester Regiment. The 1/9th and 2/9th battalions of the Manchester Regiment had been disbanded for lack of numbers. The Territorials had paid a heavy price for their brave fighting in Gallipoli, the Dardanelles, and France. It was suggested that steps should be taken to reconstitute the 9th Battalion from the remaining men of the 1/9th and 2/9th and those of the 3rd Battalion Manchester Regiment. The lists of war casualties continued to be long and tragic. Mr Joseph Hamer of Ashton had lost three of his four sons. So too had Mr and Mrs Sidebottom of Ashton, their remaining son being a prisoner-of-war.

The heavy drain of men for call-up had crippled the mining industry in England. Taking 75,000 men from the pits had resulted in a drop of 20,000,000 tons in output every year. While the needs of the army might outweigh individual needs, industry and the munitions factories had also been badly affected. It was stressed that economies in the use of coal, coke, gas and electricity were absolutely vital. Reserve stocks had been partly used and now the country could not fulfil its quota to be sent to the Allies in Europe. There had been coal mining in the Ashton district since the seventeenth century – open-cast mining at first, then colliery pits as the Industrial Revolution spread. In 1875 Ashton Moss Colliery (now beneath the site of B&Q) opened and in 1882 a second shaft was drilled to a depth of 2,850 feet (869 metres), the deepest in the world at that time. By 1918 its output of coal was severely diminished due to lack of miners. Nationally the coal shortage had become more acute and more serious than the food shortage. Gas, coal, coke and electricity would all be rationed and therefore fuel and light requisition forms would have to be issued, completed and handed in to the long suffering post office. Ashton groaned collectively. Yet more forms to fill in. Folk seem to spend half their lives filling in forms to apply for things. New ration cards were due in November so new application forms for those would have to be completed as well, especially as lard and tea were now to be officially rationed. To add insult to injury, gas prices also rose at this time. Industry received a 50 per cent discount and it was basically an exercise to regulate domestic usage. Ashton gasometers had been rebuilt after the June 1917 explosion with help from the Ministry of Munitions, and the Ashton paper grumbled that, as always, the ordinary consumer was paying the price. Gas meter rents rose as well with the Ashton Gas Company saying that meters were not cheap to install or maintain.

Peace notes had been exchanged between President Wilson of the United States and Germany since October, but there had been some who questioned the gesture. Are we ready for peace? they asked. There was a diversity of views on a peace settlement and the 'enormity of the post war social reconstruction work'. David Lloyd George had not been too far wide of the mark when he said that the Great War had been fought on grounds of business as much as anything else. However, on one issue everyone seemed to be united. The kaiser had to go. In August, the Hundred Days Offensive had begun with the Battle of Amiens. For a month from 18 September until 17 October, the Battle of the Hindenburg Line raged and, at last, the Allies managed to break through the German lines. German alliances were beginning to crumble and three weeks later they suspended their submarine warfare. On 29 October, the Croatians, Serbians and Slovenians proclaimed their own State and the next day the Ottoman Empire signed the Armistice of Mudros. At the beginning of November, Austria and Bulgaria withdrew from the war and sued for peace terms with the American President Wilson, and on 4 November, Austria-Hungary made peace with Italy and the Allies advanced to the Meuse. At last, on 9 November, Kaiser Wilhelm abdicated and Germany became a Republic. In Austria-Hungary Kaiser Charles 1st abdicated the following day. Finally 'at the eleventh hour of the eleventh day of the eleventh month' peace was declared. Ashton went wild with joy and relief. 'Flags were displayed on public buildings, shops and houses [...] work was thrown aside and the day made a holiday [...] streets were thronged and there was great jubilation [...] church bells were rung and fireworks let off [including the maroon flares intended as a daytime air raid signal warning system ...] the lights went up, the market hall clock was illuminated, there was singing of 'Tipperary' in the streets and there were scenes of delirious enthusiasm at the local military hospitals [...] the only sad note being the 1,510 Ashton men who would never come home.'

It was a celebration of the triumph of 'right over might', but tinged with sadness at the memory of so many who had selflessly made the supreme sacrifice in order that others could live in freedom. Nearly 2,500 years ago a Greek historian named Thucydides said that history was cyclical, that the same sort of things would go on happening over and over again, and so it proved to be in the case of the Great War, 'the war to end all wars'.

Just twenty years after the signing of the peace the world was once again at war, this time for six long years, to be followed by Suez, Vietnam, the Falklands, Iraq, the list goes on and on. The soldier to whom this book is especially dedicated died in the Gaza Strip and is buried in the Bethsheba War Cemetery. He died believing that he had fought in the war to end all wars but, 100 years on, the Gaza Strip is still a war zone and that is the real tragedy.

# Index